The Fighting Arts
Choosing the Way

The Fighting Arts

Choosing the Way

Compiled by
David Scott and Mick Pappas
Edited by David Scott

Rider
London Melbourne Auckland Johannesburg

Rider & Co Ltd
An imprint of Century Hutchinson Ltd
Brookmount House, 62-65 Chandos Place, Covent Garden, London WC2N 4NW

Century Hutchinson Australia (Pty) Ltd
PO Box 496, 16-22 Church Street, Hawthorn, Victoria 3122, Australia

Century Hutchinson New Zealand Ltd
PO Box 40-086, 32-34 View Road, Glenfield, Auckland 10, New Zealand

Century Hutchinson South Africa (Pty) Ltd
PO Box 337, Bergvlei 2012, South Africa

First published in Great Britain 1985
Reissue with revisions 1988

Printed and bound in Great Britain by
The Guernsey Press Co. Ltd, Guernsey, Channel Islands

British Library Cataloguing in Publication Data

Scott, David, *1944-*
The fighting arts: choosing the way.
1. Martial arts
I. Title II. Pappas, Mick
796.8

ISBN 0-7126-1085-5

Contents

Acknowledgements

David Scott and Mick Pappas wish to acknowledge their gratitude to Master Uechi and the Okinawan Uechi-Ryu Karate Board for their support in their karate training. We would also like to thank our black belt colleagues for many shared training sessions. (Special thanks to Danny.)

Contributors' Biographies

David Scott, 4th Dan

David Scott graduated with a Ph.D. from Manchester University in 1971. He is a well-known author and has published several books on foreign and health-food cookery. In 1975 he spent the year training with Master Uechi in Okinawa, Japan. He returned to England in 1976 and co-founded the Uechi-Ryu Karate-Do Association (G.B.) with Ron Ship, and opened a karate club in Liverpool which is still thriving. From 1976 to 1982 he was the Okinawan representative for Uechi-Ryu in Britain. He is interested in the traditional aspects of karate (although he doesn't object to his students practising sporting karate), the practice of Zen and its connection with the martial arts.

Mick Pappas

Mick Pappas started training in Uechi-Ryu karate in 1976 when David Scott returned from Okinawa and began teaching in Liverpool. Soon after he became Secretary of the Uechi-Ryu Karate Association (G.B.) and after visiting Okinawa in 1982 became the Okinawan Uechi-Ryu representative in Britain.

His training in Okinawa was largely spent studying and performing Uechi-Ryu kata which he believes to be the essence of his karate. Whilst in Okinawa he participated in a major commemorative karate demonstration involving masters and senior instructors from many styles. He holds the rank of third dan in Uechi-Ryu karate.

He is currently enjoying a sabbatical from his normal employment as a civil servant in order to study Philosophy at Liverpool University where he is concentrating on Philosophy of Mind, Theory of Knowledge and knowledge-based computer systems.

Harry Cook

Born in 1949 in the north-east of England, Harry Cook began studying the martial arts in 1966. Beginning with Wado Ryu karate and Aikido, he changed to Shotokan in 1968, becoming a student of Ken Smith. From 1970 to 1974 he attended the University of Durham, gaining a B.A. in Chinese and a Post-Graduate Certificate of Education. At this time he served as President of the British Universities Karate Federation (1972) and was captain of the winning Durham team in the university championships in 1973 and 1974. While at Durham he also studied Chinese internal systems under Rose Li, a leading instructor of T'ai Chi Ch'uan, Pa Kua, and Hsing I. In 1977 he left for Japan where he became a student of Okinawan Goju Ryu under Morio Higaonna, gaining a second dan in the style. While in Japan he also managed to gain some experience in Okinawan weapons, naginata, jo, and sword. Currently he holds the grades of third dan in Shotokan (JKA) and second dan in Okinawan Goju Ryu.

As well as training in the martial arts, Mr Cook also writes for a number of martial arts magazines in Britain and the USA. He has recently completed a book on Okinawan Goju Ryu.

Terry Daley

Terry Daley started karate training in 1974 after his family emigrated to Boston, USA. He trained at the Mattson Academy of Karate, which taught Uechi Ryu karate, then returned to England in 1976 and continued studying Uechi Ryu karate under Ron Ship in Shenfield, Essex. He graded to first dan in 1980, second dan in 1982 and third dan in 1984. Having opened a dojo in 1980 in London, he now has his own students of black belt standard. Selected for the England squad in 1984, he fought against the Japanese Colleges and Australia, and also represented the English Karate Federation in the USA. Also in 1984, he was a lightweight silver medallist in the English Championships.

Graham Noble

Graham Noble is at the moment researching and collecting information on karate and the martial arts for a book tracing the history of their development. He has published several articles in karate magazines. Graham has trained in both Shotokan karate and boxing. He likes to train on his own and works on karate kicks and boxing punches as well as on knee, elbow, head and other strikes. He is an individualist and has followed his own unique path in his study of the martial arts.

Alan Roberts

Born in Liverpool in 1950, Alan Roberts was educated at Madeley College and Keele University. He began studying yoga and karate at Keele in 1968, studying both Wado and Shotokan styles. He taught karate with Dr Scott in Liverpool until 1973, but now concentrates on yoga which he has taught continuously since 1971. He is a co-author of *Recipes for Living* (Wildwood House).

Introduction

This book has two purposes. The first is to provide, for both the mature student and the novice, a source of information on the forms and history of the major martial arts, on training aids and weapons systems, on the relationship between Zen and the martial arts, and finally on fitness, exercise and diet. The second purpose is to give to the person new to the martial arts the background information he or she will require to find the style, club and instructor right for his or her needs.

In the authors' opinion it is very difficult if not impossible to teach yourself a martial art; instruction in person by a qualified instructor is essential. Despite this fact most martial arts books are concerned with showing the reader in words and pictures how to practise, on his own, a particular martial art form. In our experience this type of book is impractical and usually ends up collecting dust on the buyer's bookshelves. Thus we have chosen not to provide this type of information but instead to give contact addresses, practical reference material and further reading which give the reader the opportunity to go to the source of his interest.

The book opens with a discussion of the benefits of the martial arts and is then divided into three parts.

Part One, chapter 2 explains as succinctly as possible the differences between and historical roots of each of the martial arts. Chapter 3 describes the major forms of karate and gives a short history of their individual development in the West.

Chapter 4 discusses training aids and equipment. The final chapter of this section traces the history of Zen Buddhism and its relationship to the martial arts.

Part Two of the book, chapter 6 shows the reader new to the martial arts how to find the right club; it also gives tips on behaviour and etiquette in the training hall. Chapter 7 discusses progress and development during training and points out some of the more common pitfalls. The next three chapters are useful to both the novice and the mature student. They cover a fitness and maintenance programme suitable for both getting fit and staying in condition, a discussion of all aspects of fitness and advice on diet.

Part Three, the final section of the book, is devoted to further reading and contact addresses.

Authors' note

This book was the joint idea of David Scott and Mick Pappas. The material content is shared between them and other authors they invited to contribute. David Scott and Mick Pappas are most grateful to all their co-authors and particularly to Harry Cook for his masterly contribution on the history and styles of the martial arts. This section makes up a substantial portion of the book. The book was edited by David Scott before submission to the publishers.

Part One

1 The Benefits of Martial Arts Training

Training in any martial art is essentially a process of change. A weak person is expected to become strong, while a strong person must learn to control his strength; an aggressive individual has to learn self-control, while a passive person should try to develop confidence in himself and his abilities. Some of the benefits of training in the martial arts only become apparent after a number of years of hard practice and can be understood only by those who have had similar experiences. Like Zen, it has to be done rather than talked about.

It is convenient to discuss the benefits of training one by one, but it should be remembered that to progress as a martial artist one aspect should not be stressed at the expense of the others.

Self-defence

Most of the people who begin training in the martial arts consciously or unconsciously feel that the training will improve their ability to defend themselves against physical attack. It is true that martial arts training improves an individual's speed, timing, awareness, mobility and striking ability. Sparring, although lacking certain elements of an actual fight, to some extent prepares the student for a fight by exposing him to an opponent, so enabling him to experience the nerves or 'adrenaline rush' caused by facing a higher-graded or more skilful person. To be really valuable, training should encompass both striking and grappling methods. There is no doubt that someone highly ranked in karate and judo would be able effectively to defend himself in most situations, as his ability in punching, striking and grappling will be superior to most of the attackers he is likely to face. As an example, a Japanese university lecturer and karate black belt, Mr S. Takahashi, was attacked by an armed burglar in a London hotel. According to the newspaper report (*Guardian*, 11 March 1984), he disarmed the attacker with kicks and punches and held him with an armlock until hotel security staff arrived.

A note of caution is required here; some martial arts concentrate so much on sporting or health considerations that they are no longer really effective as a method of self-defence. For example, experts in the Chinese internal systems say that they cannot be used for fighting unless the student has been training for many years and fully understands all the fine details of the art. In fact, according to some observers, the internal systems have lost any real combat value and have become methods of self-cultivation, a kind of moving yoga. While this may be true today it is also true that many of the Tai-chi-ch'uan masters of the nineteenth century successfully faced many challenges from fighters of all kinds. It is said that Yang Shao-hou (1862–1929) had problems finding training partners or students due to his habit of breaking his opponents' arms when practising pushing hands! Conversations with Western students at the headquarters of judo in Japan indicate that for some oriental teachers this attitude has not yet become extinct.

Health

Training in most of the martial arts involves improvement in strength, stamina and suppleness. At the beginning of a class it is common practice to spend five or ten minutes going through a series of exercises designed to prepare the body for training by warming up the muscles and stretching the joints. A typical warm-up would include stretching exercises such as hurdlers' splits, full splits, front bends, back bends, as well as strength- and stamina-building movements such as push-ups, sit-ups, squat thrusts, etc. These exercises, combined with the effort involved in performing the punches, kicks, locks, throws and other techniques of the martial arts, have the effect of improving the trainee's level of health and fitness.

Practice of the hard styles such as karate, taekwondo and kickboxing can also involve supplementary training such as running, skipping and weight training, all of which can improve the practitioner's health. The softer internal systems are said to aid in lowering blood pressure and nervous tension, leading to a more relaxed and stress-free life. According to one Chinese teacher, Tai-chi-ch'uan can help in treating hypertension, gastric disturbances, heart disease and tuberculosis; by stressing slow movements and relaxation it is claimed that high blood pressure can be lowered and arthritis improved by encouraging a wide range of movements. In fact, according to Miss Rose Li, a leading teacher of Chinese internal systems, Tai-chi-ch'uan is for fighting illness not for fighting men. While some of these claims have yet to be seriously investigated in the West, in mainland China Tai-chi-ch'uan is used by medical authorities as therapy for a wide range of ailments.

As well as improving physical wellbeing it is often said that the training develops a positive mental approach. There seems to be some evidence for this as research done on runners by A. H. Ismail and L. E. Tratchman at Purdue University indicates that those individuals who exercise regularly seem to show higher levels of emotional maturity, calmness and a greater ability to make accurate judgements when under pressure than those who do no training of any kind. In general, as fitness levels increased so did the individual's imagination, self-sufficiency and confidence, which manifested itself in a more positive attitude to life. This improvement was caused by the athlete facing and overcoming difficult physical and psychological tasks. In the martial arts the student faces a whole series of difficult tasks which he tries to overcome not only in the dojo but in his daily life. This is one of the values of the grading system which clearly defines the task and provides visible proof of success. The student is expected to learn a number of lessons from this, the most important being that success comes from his own efforts and hard work and that he sets his own limits and restrictions. This is why many instructors are sparing in their praise; they do not want the students to accept less than perfection. Kenran Umeiji, a master of kyudo (Japanese archery), made the point very clearly when he said:

> For what ultimately matters in learning archery or any other art is not what comes out of it but what goes into it. Into, that is into the person. The self-practice in the service of an outward accomplishment serves, beyond it, the development of the inner man. And what endangers this inner development more than anything else? Standing still in his achievement. A man must go on increasing, endlessly increasing.

Sport

Competition or sport karate provides an opportunity to compete against other karate-ka from different areas and styles; this is also true of judo, kendo, taekwondo and those Chinese styles which have developed a competitive approach. This aspect of the martial arts has become more and more popular; in fact, for some individuals competition success is the sole reason for training. Competition usually takes the form of sparring with a restricted range of techniques being applied to a limited number of targets. Thus in judo some of the most effective self-defence techniques are no longer practised as they are illegal in judo tournaments; in karate the same situation may be found. Those who are successful can go on to represent their association or country in world championships. While the modern trend is to place a great deal of emphasis and importance on the sporting approach, it must be remembered that it is only one part of a much greater whole. Approached in the right way, competitions can be valuable as testing grounds for both the physical and the psychological development of the student and can help with his or her overall progress. Many instructors are of the opinion that entering competitions is a valuable step in training, but eventually it must be left behind as the student matures.

If a beginner in the martial arts wants to enter competitions on a regular basis he should study judo, karate or kendo, but not aikido or those classical Chinese systems which have no sporting function.

Self-discipline

All oriental martial arts are considered to be more than simple physical skills. According to the founders and leading teachers of these systems, simply practising technique is not enough to achieve mastery. The student must strive to improve the moral and spiritual qualities of his life, constantly facing his own weaknesses and inadequacies with a view to self-improvement. This approach is usually known as 'the way' (*do* in Japanese, *tao* in Chinese), and is derived from the teachings of Zen Buddhism, Taoism, Confucius and Mencius. The most famous example of this way of life is known as bushido (the way of the warrior) which was the code of honour followed by the Japanese samurai. It stresses responsibility for one's actions, respect between seniors and juniors, duty, honesty, obligation and the development of a strong spirit. While these values may seem old-fashioned or excessive by modern standards, it is vital to maintain them, as without them there would be little or no morality to the martial arts, so allowing self-indulgence and brutality free rein. It is the responsibility of all instructors to teach not only technique but also the correct attitudes which are an integral part of the martial arts. It is most important to realize that the martial arts are not about developing well-trained thugs. Gichin Funakoshi, the creator of Shotokan karate-do, summed it up when he said: 'Karate begins and ends with courtesy.'

According to Funakoshi, the ideal martial artist was 'the man of Tao', whom he contrasted to the opposite, which he called 'the little man'. When asked to explain the difference, Funakoshi said that when the little man gains his first dan he runs home and tells everyone. Upon gaining second dan he climbs to the rooftops and shouts out the news, and on gaining third dan he drives around the city in his car broadcasting his success. In comparison, the man of Tao on gaining first dan bows his head. Upon receiving second dan he bows his head and shoulders, and on receiving third dan he bows from the waist and walks away. This approach contrasts strongly with the ego-building characteristics of the modern approach to sport. As one old Okinawan karate teacher is reported to have said, 'In the past you did karate for yourself; now you do it for everyone else.'

2 Martial Arts of the World

From the earliest times man and his primitive ancestors have had to fight to survive. As long as monkeys and apes continued to dwell in the trees the best form of defence was flight; on the open plains this was often not a realistic option. Our early ancestors attempted to solve the problem in two ways: by organizing into strong groups or tribes for mutual protection, and by codifying the knowledge and experience of combat into systems which could be taught to the next generation, so improving their chances of survival when faced with a dangerous enemy, whether animal or human. Charles Darwin stated this very clearly in *On the Origin of Species*: 'The slightest advantage or better adaption in one being over those with which it comes into competition, in however slight a degree, will turn the balance.'

Over the centuries many methods evolved, some based on strength and ferocity and others based on more subtle and sophisticated approaches. In practical terms it is convenient to classify all systems into one of three types, according to the dominant characteristic of the method: kicking and punching systems, grappling systems and weapons systems.

Of course, many martial arts utilize all three approaches, but in practice one aspect tends to dominate. There is also the modern development of combat sports where survival is not the keynote; the practitioner seeks to score points in a mock combat or perform according to some aesthetic ideal. In this general survey of the martial arts some of the sporting systems are included as it is a fact that many so-called combat sports are as effective as the classical systems in a real fight due to the intensity and severity of the training.

India

India has one of the oldest cultures in the world, with a long military tradition as well as the more gentle art of yoga. It is no surprise that India is a rich source of knowledge on combat methods. The sixty-four arts (*catuhsasti-kala*) required of a nobleman in ancient India included physical culture (*vyay-amavidya*), and use of weapons (*ayudha*).

Kicking and punching systems

Kalaripayit This term means 'battlefield training' and is used to describe a system of fighting practised in the south of India. There are two major styles: the northern and the southern, which, although related, do have distinct features.

Northern kalaripayit This style is practised in a building 14 metres long by 7 metres wide, with the floor 1 metre below ground level. The building belongs to the teacher, who often uses it as a surgery and massage room. Like most teachers of combat, kalari masters do not see their methods as simply destructive, for the same knowledge can be used to heal as well as destroy. The northern style is characterized by high jumping and kicking techniques, low stances and open, expansive movements. This energetic approach demands a high level of conditioning which the trainees acquire by a wide range of methods. Before a student can begin training he is subjected to an extensive massage which lasts for thirty minutes a day for one month. Once a student begins training he also practises an extensive set of stretching and strength-building exercises such as sit-ups and push-ups. One unusual exercise is known as the 'crocodile walk' in which the practitioners move across the ground with a hopping or jumping action using only their hands and toes to propel themselves backwards and forwards.

Southern kalaripayit Usually practised outside, the southern style is characterized by circular movements, open-hand blocks and strikes and close-in techniques. The kicks are lower and not as flamboyant as in the northern style. Stances are higher and feature a more powerful use of the arms and shoulders. The southern style also makes extensive use of throws and trips meshed with the various strikes.

In both styles progression follows the same sequence: (1) unarmed training, (2) training with bamboo or rattan weapons, (3) training with edged steel weapons, (4) learning how to attack the vital points. This last aspect is the most secret and is known as *marma-adi*. In most cases the weapons tactics follow those of the empty hand.

The techniques employed by both styles feature open-hand strikes and blows as well as the clenched fist. Kicking methods are centred on the front and roundhouse kicks, although a type of side kick is seen. Defence is based on agile movements to evade an attack meshed with deflections using the forearm.

As well as sparring and strength training, the student of kalaripayit also practises formal exercises which include the full range of attacks and defences used in the style.

Muki boxing Classical works such as the *Rig Veda* mention fights between the heroes and their enemies in which fists are the weapons used. In the *Ramayana* of Valmiki, Dundubhee is killed by Vali in such a fight. Although almost extinct due to the popularity of Western boxing (introduced in the 1890s), one of the old systems has survived and is now practised in Benares. Individual fights are held once a year, with no restrictions as to targets (except attacks to the groin); injuries are severe and frequent. It is said that a skilled muki boxer can break stones and coconuts with his hands.

Vajra musti A system of fighting which features grappling methods as well as punching. The impact of the punches is increased by wearing the *vajra musti*, a knuckleduster-like implement which can inflict serious injury. This style barely survives today due to its severity. A variant of the *vajra musti* is known as the *baghnak*, or tiger's claw. It consists of a metal bar with two rings welded on either end which fit over the index and little fingers. Several curved and sharpened claws are fastened to the bar in such a way that they are hidden by the fingers. In use they duplicate the ripping and tearing actions of a tiger's claws. According to one observer in the nineteenth century who saw the *baghnak* in use:

> The nude combatants were armed with 'tiger's claws' of horn; formerly when these were of steel, the death of one of the athletes was unavoidable. The weapons, fitted into a kind of handle, were fastened by thongs to the closed right hand. The men, drunk with Bhang or Indian hemp, rushed upon each other and tore like tigers at face and body; forehead-skins would hang in shreds; necks and ribs would be laid open, and not infrequently one or both would bleed to death.

Grappling systems

Kusti India has long been famous for the skill of its wrestlers. The name *kusti* is a general term which refers to a wide range of styles and methods. Other terms used in the past are *malla-krida*, *malla-yuddha* and *niyuddha-krida*.

The modern style of wrestling seen today in India resembles western freestyle wrestling, in that a wide range of throwing techniques are incorporated with groundwork and locks. It is probable that the groundwork and locks were introduced by Moslem soldiers in the thirteenth and fourteenth centuries. There seems to have been some connection between the techniques used by Moslem wrestlers in India and the methods used by their co-religionists in the Persian Zoorkhaneh – 'Houses of Power' – where wrestling and strength-building methods have been taught for centuries. Hinduism also contributed to the development of kusti; at the end of the seventeenth century, Ramdas, the father of Indian athletics, travelled the country exhorting his fellow Hindus to develop strength and fighting skill as a tribute to the monkey god Hanuman, the devoted ally of the great Rama in his struggle with the demon Rakshasa (this tale is set out in the great epic poem, the

Ramayana). Wrestling became very popular and contributed to the martial spirit of the various Indian kingdoms.

Wrestling suffered a decline with the coming of the British and the subsequent loss of royal patronage. However, the nineteenth century saw the emergence of famous Moslem and Hindu wrestlers. One of the strongest was Sadika, who is said to have killed an ass with a single blow. Probably the greatest wrestler was Ghulam Mohammed, more usually known as Gama. Born in 1878, he became the unchallenged champion of India. In 1910 he fought B. F. (Doc) Roller, one of the great American wrestlers, in London, breaking some of Roller's ribs in the process. One month later he faced Stanislaus Zbyszko, the finest Graeco-Roman wrestler in Europe, who survived the match by staying on the ground and refusing to fight! Sixteen years later a rematch was arranged by the Maharajah of Patalia. Zbyszko was defeated in six seconds!

The great skill of Indian wrestlers is simply explained: they train with total devotion and intensity. The routine they follow, which is at least two centuries old, consists of rigorous exercise and a well-balanced diet, high in protein and fresh vegetables. The exercises consist of running, swimming, lifting heavy stones and logs, as well as wrestling. All wrestlers practise *baithaks* (squats) and *dands* (cat stretches) to develop strength and stamina. Up to four thousand *baithaks* and *dands* are done per day. A unique form of training, known as *malkhamb* (which means 'a pole for the use of a wrestler'), is also used by some wrestlers. Basically the wrestler uses a flexible rattan cane which is hung from a hook. The wrestler then practises various throwing and locking techniques on the cane to improve his style. The cane is also used to strengthen the muscles of the body by providing resistance to the movement. A very rare book, *Cane and Wrestling* by Anant Harihar Khasgiwale, published in Poona in 1928, details the complete system.

Although many would say that wrestling is not really a martial art, more of a sport, it is recorded that one Indian wrestler, Balambhat Dada, asked his opponents to sign a document releasing each party from responsibility in the case of injury or death. He did this after several of his opponents vomited blood and died due to the severity of his wrestling technique.

Cheena-adi This is a modern eclectic system taught in Ceylon. It is based on techniques derived from Indian wrestling and stick fighting, and shows some influence of Japanese ju-jutsu and Chinese grappling (chin-na) methods. The leading teacher in the 1950s was R. A. Vairamuttu.

Weapons systems

As mentioned above, India has a long tradition of martial prowess. Before the establishment of British rule in India many of the local princes were in a state of almost permanent war with their neighbours. The military skills of races such as the Sikhs, Rajputs and Mahrattas were established and developed through this long period of internecine warfare. The range of weapons used was enormous and included swords, spears, bows and arrows, axes, knives, as well as the use of cavalry and fighting elephants. Although the use of these weapons on the battlefield has ended, some of them are still used and taught by the kalaripayit masters.

The stick The stick or staff is often the easiest weapon to begin training with. It has many advantages over a sharp steel weapon in that it is cheap, easily accessible, durable and effective enough in skilled hands to be a lethal weapon. The stick, or *lathi*, is used by the Indian police to control crowds and break up riots. There are many different ways to use the stick, including holding it at one end and using it in a flicking action like a whip. According to one report, a young boy earned his living on the Bombay dockside by inviting tourists to throw stones at him; he used his *lathi* to deflect the stones before they could hit him. According to a report published in the *Sunday Times* (21 October 1984), the *lathi* is still used to lethal effect. Two railway employees started fighting after a heavy drinking bout. One of them, Sri Appa Rao, struck the other, Sri Ramana Rao, with a *lathi*, killing him instantly. According to a report in an Indian newspaper, the *Swadrin Patrika*, 'a gloominess cast its shadow in the house of Ramana Rao'!

In South India training with the stick is known as *silambam*, and includes weapons ranging in size from 15 centimetres to 2 metres. Recently there has been a movement to modify the stick-fighting techniques to produce a competitive sport, but this is resisted by the older instructors who want to preserve the traditional combat value of the weapon. Training with the *lathi* centres on form training followed by prearranged sparring and free sparring with the master. Certain games are sometimes used to develop skill, one of which is to attack peeled bananas set on sticks in a set pattern: this develops hand–eye coordination and accuracy and resembles the type of sabre practice used in the West to train cavalrymen.

The sword Indian swords display a wide and strange variety of designs, compared with the more conservative Western weapon. This is not a matter of chance or fashion, as the wide varieties of techniques available often determined the design of the blade. Certain basic types can, however, be seen; they include the *talwar*, a weapon based on Persian prototypes, and which features a slightly curved blade with a broadened point. The *khanda* is a straight double-edged weapon with a slightly broadened point, while the Madrasi straight sword has a narrower blade coming to a sharp point. Possibly the most interesting type is the *pata*, which was developed by the Maratha warriors. This weapon features a flexible double-edged blade, usually of European manufacture, and a gauntlet hilt. The swordsman holds a transverse grip in his fist so that the sword is an extension of his forearm. The *pata* is difficult to use and is the province of the expert swordsman only. It is generally agreed that it is the most effective of all the Indian swords as it is wielded by the strong muscles of the forearm, and not the wrist.

One type of sword, which seems to be a cross between a sword and a whip, is the *urumi*, or spring sword. It is made from a number of flexible ribbons of metal about 2 metres long. These are sharpened on both edges and joined at one end to a wooden hilt. Normally kept coiled, the *urumi* is quickly whipped out and used in a series of curves to attack and defend. In the hands of anyone other than an expert it would be more dangerous to the user than his enemy.

A common type of short sword or dagger is known as the Bundi dagger. It has a short triangular double-edged blade with a handle resembling that of the *pata*. It is used in close combat and is often delivered with a straight punching movement. Some Bundi daggers have thickened points to allow them to penetrate chain mail or light body armour.

Training with the sword follows the same pattern as the stick. Skills developed with wooden weapons are easily transferred to steel.

There is also a variety of throwing weapons taught, including some which are burning when thrown. Probably the most effective is the *chakram* or war quoit – a steel disc weighing 8 ounces, with a diameter of 6 inches or so. The outer edge is sharpened to a razor thinness and the weapon is thrown at the target with an action resembling that of a frisbee. The *chakram* may be regarded as an unusual variant of the throwing axe.

China

China is generally considered by martial arts historians to have been the birthplace of most of the martial arts in the world today. In the course of its long history China has produced many thousands of fighting systems, created by soldiers, monks, scholars and peasants. It is often a matter of great pride to followers of Okinawan, Japanese, Korean and Indonesian systems that their schools are rooted in China, and in fact many modern systems fabricate histories with Chinese connections for reasons of prestige.

Kicking and punching systems

Chinese boxing, generally known as ch'uan-fa (fist way), guo-shu (national art) or wu-shu (martial art), can be readily classified into two major groups:

(a) the external (wai-chia), often known as Shaolin Temple boxing;

(b) the internal (nei-chia), most commonly represented by Tai-chi-ch'uan, the soft dance-like system sometimes called shadow boxing.

The external systems are classified by fast muscular movements stressing rapid punching and kicking techniques, whereas the internal uses slow movements stressing posture, breathing and the use of intrinsic power, or *ch'i*. The term kung-fu means skilled performance and does not only refer to martial arts.

Shaolin Temple boxing *(Shaolin-ssu Ch'uan-fa)* According to tradition, this form of fighting was taught to the monks in the Shaolin Temple by the great Zen master Bodhidharma. He taught them the basis of a fighting system to strengthen their bodies and minds. After he died (AD 527), he left two books, the I Chin Ching (Muscle Change Classic) and the Hsi Sui Ching (Marrow Washing Classic), which contained the essence of his teachings. From this background emerged a system known as the Shih-pa-lo-han-shou (Eighteen Lohan Hands) which formed the basis of Shaolin Temple boxing.

An interesting story, but unfortunately not one word of it is true, although it is repeated time after time by most followers of the martial arts! There is a Shaolin Temple, situated on Mount Sung in Honan Province, which was a centre for fighting arts, and Bodhidharma did live in the Shaolin as a meditation master. These are verifiable facts, but the rest of the tale was created to give the fighting art a famous founder and thus gain prestige over other systems.

The styles known as Shaolin in China now are many and various. The northern methods use long open movements with high kicks and gymnastic jumping and rolling movements; the modern mainland system known as wu-shu, which is not a fighting method but a form of gymnastics, is based to some extent on these systems. The southern versions of Shaolin feature upright postures, low kicks to the groin and knee, and the use of the open hand. These systems have managed to retain more combat effectiveness than many of the mainland methods by being exported to Chinese communities overseas, so avoiding control by the mainland government. Many of the Shaolin systems are named after animals, such as the Tiger style (Hu Ch'uan), Praying Mantis (T'ang Lang), Dragon style (Lung Ch'uan), Phoenix (Fung Ch'uan), and White Crane (Pai Hao) – usually the techniques resemble to some extent the animal the style is named after. For example, the White Crane style features blocking actions which resemble the opening movements of a crane's wings, while the Tiger style uses claw-like movements of the hands.

The most famous style however was named after its founder, a Buddhist nun – Wing Chun. This style, prevalent in Hong Kong, was that favoured by Bruce Lee before he created Jeet-kune-do. The style features a turned-in stance with the body facing forwards; the hands protect the body's centre line and attack the opponent from close in. Wing Chun may be regarded as a good basic example of southern Shaolin.

The internal systems (nei-chia) are based on a totally different approach to that of the Shaolin methods. Unlike the Shaolin boxers, they do not train for physical strength by lifting stone weights or punching wooden targets; rather, the internal stylist aims for a soft evasive technique resembling the action of moving water which instantly adapts to its conditions, or the movements of clouds or smoke blown by the wind, so insubstantial that it cannot be seized. The internal styles have been influenced to a great extent by the theories and concepts of Taoism, which seeks to promote a harmony between man and nature. Muscular power is not stressed, the student develops his *ch'i* or intrinsic power by harmonizing his mind and spirit with the great cosmic *ch'i* of the universe. Mastery is reached when the individual ego becomes one with the universe.

There are three basic internal styles, although others do exist:

Tai-chi-ch'uan Probably the most widely practised method in China, Tai-chi-ch'uan (supreme ultimate boxing) is said to have been created by the Taoist immortal Chang San-feng, a twelfth-century recluse who lived in the Wu-tang mountains, in Hupeh Province. He is said to have witnessed a fight between a snake and a crane, in which the crane's stabbing attack with its beak was neutralized by the snake's twisting elusive movements. He saw in this struggle living proof of the Taoist belief stated in the *Tao Te Ching* by the ancient master, Lao Tzu: 'The most yielding of things in the universe overcomes the most hard' (*Tao Te Ching*, verse 43).

Inspired by this, Chang San-feng created Tai-chi-ch'uan. This story is almost certainly untrue, but, like the tale of Bodhidharma, it seems to survive against mere facts, probably because, as a teaching story, it exemplifies the essence of Tai-chi-ch'uan. The truth of the matter seems to be that the roots of the style were in Chen village, Honan Province. It passed to Yang Lu-chan who founded the Yang style. The style was passed down through the family until Yang Cheng-fu (1883–1935) took the style to south China. One of his students, Cheng Man-ch'ing, became the leading teacher of the Yang style and co-authored with Robert W. Smith the first useful English language work on the subject, *T'ai Chi: The Supreme Ultimate Exercise for Health, Sport and Self-Defense* (Tuttle, Vermont, 1967).

Apart from the Yang, there are other styles of Tai-chi-ch'uan, including the Chen village style, the Sun style (founded by Sun Lu-t'ang, 1859–1933) and the Wu (founded by Wu Chien-ch'uan, 1870–1942). There is also a modern synthetic style of Tai-chi-ch'uan developed on the mainland which is gaining in popularity.

Although the styles may look slightly different, they are all based on the same principles and use the same techniques and movements. The differences tend to be based on various instructors' tastes; for example, Sun Lu-tang liked to use small tight movements in a high stance, while the Yang style is marked by long flowing movements in deep stances.

Some flavour of Tai-chi-ch'uan may be gained from the following advice taken from the *Tai-chi-ch'uan Classics*, probably written by Wu Ho-ching in the nineteenth century:

> One should yield at the opponent's slightest pressure and adhere to him at his slightest retreat.
>
> The entire body is so sensitive that not a feather will be able to be added and so pliable that a fly cannot alight on it without setting it in motion.
>
> Use the mind to move the *ch'i* with quiet effort, in order to store the *ch'i* in the bones.
>
> Keep the stomach relaxed and calm; the *ch'i* is stored in the bones. The spirit is calm and the body peaceful, be aware of the direction of the mind.

Tai-chi-ch'uan can also be performed with a sword; the tactics used follow exactly those used by the empty hand and so should be regarded simply as an extension of the empty-hand art.

Pa-kua Named after the symbols found in the *I Ching (Book of*

Changes), Pa-kua shares the same theoretical and philosophical concepts as Tai-chi-ch'uan. Its founder is unknown, but the art came to prominence in the Ch'ing dynasty due to the activities of Tung Hai-ch'uan (1798–1879). The stories about him are many and varied, but they all indicate that he was a fighter of tremendous ability. He is said to have defeated a group of men all armed with weapons without any injury to himself. It is said that in middle age he became a eunuch in the Emperor's palace to avoid the legal consequences of some of his activities. Pa-kua is based on circling movements using the palms to intercept and deflect an incoming attack. Stress is always placed on movement and adapting to change, while never meeting a force head on. Training in pa-kua concentrates on 'walking the circle', the practitioner moving rapidly in a tight circle while practising the various manoeuvres of the palm.

Pa-kua also makes use of the sword, the long knife and the spear. There is also a special knife unique to pa-kua, known as the semicircular sword, which is very effective if used close in.

Hsing-i The third of the internal systems is known as hsing-i (the form of the mind boxing) and was created by Chi Lung-feng at the beginning of the seventeenth century. The system is based on five basic actions, quite direct in application. They are: splitting (p'i-ch'uan), crushing (peng-ch'uan), drilling (tsuan-ch'uan), pounding (p'ao-ch'uan) and crossing (heng-ch'uan).

These basic techniques are amplified and expanded with movements based on animals such as the horse, monkey, tiger, bear, dragon, etc. Of all the internal methods, hsing-i looks most like the more common external Shaolin schools. Hsing-i is said to have produced the strongest fighters of all the internal methods, men such as Shang Yun-hsiang (1863–1938), who is said to have killed some of his opponents.

The internal systems are generally taught together, with the student starting with Tai-chi-ch'uan, then progressing through pa-kua to hsing-i. The leading teachers of these systems as combat forms are Wang Shu-chin and Hung I-hsiang, both of whom live in Taiwan. In Britain Miss Rose Li is probably one of the most knowledgeable teachers.

Chinese systems are in a state of evolution at the moment. Many of them have been strongly influenced by karate and taekwondo, especially in the adoption of high kicks and grading systems. The poor showing of Hong Kong fighters against Thai boxers has led to a critical re-evaluation of the traditional methods.

Grappling systems

Shuai-chiao The Chinese style of wrestling, *shuai-chiao*, employs most of the techniques used by wrestlers all over the world. It has its origins in training methods used by soldiers and in a game known as *chiao-ti*, in which contestants wore cow horns on their heads and butted one another! Certainly by the time of the T'ang dynasty (AD 618–897) wrestling was highly developed, although nowadays it seems to have stagnated to some extent. In contests between practitioners of Japanese judo and Chinese shuai-chiao, the Chinese stylists have come off poorly. This will of course change as the style spreads and becomes more competitive, as it will be exposed to a wide variety of techniques and training systems.

Shuai-chiao practitioners wear a jacket and belt somewhat like judo or Russian sambo fighters. The best wrestler on Taiwan is Shang Tung-sheng, who, according to R. W. Smith, is such a rough fighter that he can hold his own against anybody. Within the last few years Shang Tung-sheng has started teaching his approach to shuai-chiao in the USA. Such exposure should result in a rapid technical improvement.

Shuai-chiao does not use chokes or groundwork. However, there are more complete styles of wrestling practised by the minority peoples who have preserved their own distinct systems. These methods, as well as foreign systems practised in China such as Mongolian wrestling and Graeco-Roman style, could aid in the future development of shuai-chiao.

Ch'in-na This is the art of seizing an opponent and twisting his limbs to throw or control him. Ch'in-na techniques are taught in all systems of boxing and are obviously an important part of wrestling. Some teachers have specialized in this, and so it may also be considered a system in itself. Students of this art must first acquire a wide knowledge of anatomy in order to apply best the painful locks to the arms and wrist. Some styles of Chinese boxing are famous for their skills in ch'in-na, perhaps the most well known is the ying-chao (eagle claw) system. Students of this method build strength in the hands and arms by grasping weighted jars, twisting bamboos and doing a large number of push-ups on the fingers. As the techniques of ch'in-na set out to control the opponent rather than injure him, they are most suitable for police work. The leading teacher of ch'in-na on Taiwan is Han Ch'ing-t'ang.

Weapons systems

Almost all schools of Chinese boxing teach the use of a variety of weapons, some of which are generally available, such as the knife or staff, and others which are unique to one particular style. There are also weapons systems which developed without any reference to empty-hand fighting. It is impossible to describe all the available weapons and systems here – that would take a series of books in itself – but it is fair to say that the following weapons are widely used:

The sword There are two basic types: the *chien*, which is a straight, double-edged weapon, and the *tao*, which has a heavy single-edged curved blade. Expert swordsmen employ a wide range of techniques, including straight thrusting movements and curved slashing cuts. The style of fighting employed by these swordsmen was observed by an Englishman, Thomas Meadows, who was in China in the 1850s. He wrote:

> Another man, who was armed with a sword and rattan buckler, without being so manifestly angry, was much louder and more voluble in his abuse. He accompanied it with a selection of those curious pranks that the Chinese sword-and-buckler man executes in the course of his parade exercises, – such as springing with his equipment into the air and performing a sword cut and a loud yell when up there; then suddenly squatting down under the shelter of his buckler – in an attitude that a stiff-jointed and tight-breeched European would be in vain to imitate – and doing a severe cut from underneath at the legs of an imaginary foe: then again, placing the buckler, still attached to his arm, on the ground, putting his head on the centre and tumbling over and over with it in the direction of his (still) imaginary opponent.

Such methods can still be seen today in a demonstration of Chinese swordsmanship. There are also swords with hooked ends or strangely curved blades which are used in specialized ways.

The staff A favourite weapon of Chinese martial arts, the staff (*kuen*) comes in a wide variety of forms. There are specialized techniques using the short, long or jointed staff. There are also historical references to exceptionally strong fighters who used staffs made of iron.

Probably the staff began as a peasant weapon, but it soon developed a highly sophisticated technique. It is interesting to note that the Shaolin monks were famous for the quality of their staff skills. Ch'eng Chung-tou wrote a book on the Shaolin staff method in the sixteenth century.

Spears of various kinds and halberds are also used by the boxing schools, and were the favoured weapons of the Society of Righteous and Harmonious Fists (the Boxers) in their rising at the end of the nineteenth century.

As well as the weapons mentioned above, there is a bewildering array of axes, knives, chains, clubs and throwing weapons used by Chinese martial artists. The modern wu-shu teams from mainland China often feature some of these weapons in their demonstrations. Certainly on the mainland combat use of these weapons has declined and has been replaced with gymnastic exhibitions, but many styles based in Hong Kong, Taiwan and Singapore continue to teach weapons in the traditional manner.

Japan

Hachiman, the Japanese god of war, exemplified all the traditional martial virtues: courage, loyalty and duty. His followers, the samurai, the warrior class of Japan, dominated Japanese culture for over a thousand years. The duty of a samurai was to fight and die for his *daimyo* (lord) when necessary. The stern code by which he lived his life was known as Bushido (the Way of the Warrior), part of which was the acquisition and lifelong practice of martial skills. This led to the formation of *ryu*, schools of martial tradition where a young samurai could be taught how to fight skilfully and how to die bravely if and when the time came. All effective weapons and fighting techniques were taught. By the seventeenth century there were over 9000 *ryu* teaching over sixty different fighting systems. Some combat methods were developed by monks, peasants and merchants in reaction to the samurai's dominant position. The famous warrior-monks, or *sohei*, situated on Mount Hiei, near Kyoto, developed methods of spear and halberd fighting to defend their land and wealth against samurai clans.

Kicking and punching systems

Due to the emphasis on weapons techniques there are no ancient schools which developed empty-hand striking as the primary means of combat. However, there were methods which employed strikes as part of their total system. According to the *Nihon Shoki* treatise, in 23 BC two champion wrestlers, Nomi no Sukune and Taima no Kehaya, fought before the Emperor Suinin. Sukune won the fight by first breaking Kehaya's ribs with a kick and then trampling on his legs. Later Kehaya died of his injuries.

Karate-do Karate-do (empty-hand way) entered Japan only at the beginning of this century. Karate was actually created in Okinawa, a culture which at times owed allegiance to China rather than Japan. In the 1920s a group of Okinawan masters introduced their systems to Japan; men such as Gichin Funakoshi (Shotokan), Kenwa Mabuni (Shito Ryu), Choki Motobu (Shorin Ryu), Kanei Uechi* (Uechi Ryu) and Chojun Miyagi (Goju Ryu) taught the first generation of Japanese instructors who went on to develop a distinctive Japanese style of karate.

All Japanese styles of karate are characterized by precise disciplined movements; perfection of form is valued as an end in itself and, indeed, mastery of karate is traditionally seen in the perfect execution of the *kata* (formal exercises), although, with the introduction of competition fighting, kata are either being

* son of Konbun Uechi.

neglected or are distorted in order to be more aesthetically pleasing. Punching techniques are usually linear, with a stop–go type of motion, whereas kicking techniques use many circular or semicircular motions. The discipline in the *dojo* (training hall) is strict, with particular attention paid to the *kohai-sempai* (junior–senior) relationships of the members. The instructor (*sensei*) is central to the dojo and it is expected that students will show him respect at all times. In a traditional dojo the students train by practising *kihon-waza* (basic techniques), kata and various types of *kumite* (sparring). Power and impact is developed by using the *makiwara* (striking post), and stamina is improved by intensive calisthenics. Karate is not regarded solely as a method of fighting, but is also regarded as a *shugyo,* or austere discipline, intended to improve the moral qualities of its students. This is most strongly stressed in the maxims of Gichin Funakoshi, the father of Japanese karate, the most important of which is: '*Karate ni sentenashi*' – (There is no first attack in karate).

Shorinji kempo Shorinji kempo is the Japanese reading of the Chinese Shaolin Temple boxing (see above). This style was introduced into Japan by Michiomi Nakano in 1947. Nakano, better known as Doshin So, was an agent of the Japanese government in China during the war. He studied various Chinese fighting arts, eventually becoming the student of Wen Lao-shi, a teacher of northern Shaolin boxing. According to Doshin So, he was appointed Wen Lao-shi's successor in 1936, so becoming head of the Shaolin system. This story is questioned by martial arts historians, as there is no evidence from Chinese sources to validate these claims.

As well as his exposure to Chinese methods, Doshin So also studied ju-jutsu under Yoshiharu Okuyama, master of the Hakko Ryu. It was by combining the ju-jutsu methods with Chinese kempo that he created his own martial art, which he named Nippon Shorinji kempo.

Technically, the art, as taught by Doshin So, was composed of 610 techniques, involving punches, kicks, locks and throws. Once the basics have been absorbed, training concentrates on prearranged sparring methods with a partner, leading to free sparring in armour, although Doshin So never emphasized competitive sparring as an end in itself. He regarded Shorinji kempo and its associated school of Kongo Zen as a way of developing the spiritual and moral qualities of his students. One of his senior students, Shigeru Uchiyama, expressed the essence of Shorinji kempo thus:

> Shorinji Kempo is not aimed at winning victories, but through the spiritual training received, an unchallengeable spiritual power is developed. Love that which is right and just, and in achieving happiness, do not forget the other person's happiness. This is the true aim of Shorinji Kempo practice.

Nippon kempo In the 1930s many Japanese karate-ka were experimenting with new, sometimes radical, training systems. The Okinawan techniques as taught by Funakoshi, Miyagi, Motobu and others were examined in the light of experience gained from Japanese martial arts, especially kendo. Instructors such as Tatsuo Yamada, Kenwa Mabuni and Hironori Otsuka began to develop sparring methods, Yamada and Mabuni going so far as to wear armour to allow contact when sparring. There are photographs of students at Tokyo University karate club wearing armour while sparring. Out of the experience gained from this type of training, Masaru Sawayama, a university student, created Nippon kempo, a system which concentrates on sparring while wearing body armour, a helmet and gloves. Full-power blows are not permitted as the aim is to score points rather than knockouts. Ground fighting and grappling is permitted, and is taught within the syllabus of the art. As with all Japanese systems, the art is seen to be more than mere fighting and great importance is placed on developing the correct attitudes of respect and self-control. The apparent violence of the fighting must be transcended before the real benefits of the art are felt.

One system strongly influenced by Nippon kempo is toshu kakuto, a method of fighting developed by Sanshu Chiba for the Japanese Self-Defence Force. This method is a synthesis of techniques derived from kempo, judo, karate, boxing and wrestling. It has no sporting applications as it is intended for military use; it is, in fact, the Japanese equivalent of close-quarter combat.

Grappling systems

Sumo Sumo is a type of wrestling practised in one form or another for the past 2000 years. In its original form it seems to have included kicking and striking, as it was intended as one of the training methods for a warrior. The two and a half centuries of peace imposed by the Tokugawa shogunate (1603–1867) led to the establishment of sumo as a grappling sport practised by professionals. There are about forty techniques commonly used, although the Sumo Association lists over seventy. The wrestlers are usually very big and heavy with tremendous strength and endurance. Most of the throws are applied by seizing the opponent's loincloth or belt, known as a *mawashi*, and throwing him out of the fighting area (*dohyo*), or pushing him to the ground. There is no groundwork in sumo, and the matches are usually over in a short time. The grand champions or *yokozuna* would be formidable opponents for any fighter. In 1895 W. K. Burton observed the grand champion of the day: 'The man would be looked on as an enormous fellow anywhere in the world. He is 6 ft 4 ins high, in bare feet, measures 48½ ins round the chest, and weighs 400 lbs.'

The rigorous training of a professional sumo wrestler takes place in a *beya*, or 'stable', an institution which combines the functions of gymnasium and hostel. A young apprentice wrestler learns his art from the senior wrestlers while also acting as cleaner, cook and personal servant for the older wrestlers. The young wrestlers begin practising very early – at four or five in the morning, giving way to the seniors at seven or eight. The huge size of the wrestlers is brought about by their diet which is centred on a stew known as *chanko-nabe*. Some wrestlers lift weights to develop power, while all of them practise a method known as *teppo*, which consists of slamming their bodies and hands against wooden pillars. Flexibility is cultivated in order to lower the centre of gravity to avoid being thrown.

Ju-jutsu The first Japanese fighting art taught in the West, ju-jutsu may be regarded as a relative of sumo. The 'art of flexibility' was part of the training of a classical *bushi* or samurai, and involved using grappling and striking methods when disarmed or when minimally armed. To the samurai it was a last-ditch technique, used only when no other weapon was available. During the Tokugawa period, combat effectiveness became less important and many schools of ju-jutsu developed, often basing their technique on abstract Chinese neo-Confucian or Taoist concepts. Effective techniques were ignored in favour of aesthetic considerations. The concept of 'giving way' to an attack and the idea that 'softness overcomes strength' were stressed, producing a harmonious performance, undisturbed by excessive strength. This viewpoint was put forward by William Bankier, a student of Yukio Tani, one of the first teachers of the art in Britain:

> One thing upon which you must concentrate your mind at the outset is to learn how to move about gracefully and easily. The more gracefully you can glide about, the better chance you have of prolonging the contest. If you move awkwardly you will tire quickly. There are only two simple rules to be observed: first move quickly; secondly never use force. Make your opponent exert all the force he likes, but preserve your own strength and energy.

There has been a revival of interest in ju-jutsu in Britain over the last few years and the art now claims many followers. The majority of the systems practised today owe little to traditional Japanese ju-jutsu and are based largely on judo, with additions from karate, aikido and Western wrestling. For example, it is quite common to see British ju-jutsu practitioners training with weapons derived from Okinawan systems, such as the *sai*, *tonfa* and *nunchaku*. These weapons owe more to the Chinese cinema industry than the martial arts.

Judo According to Jigoro Kano (1860–1938), judo is 'the way of gentleness, or of first giving way in order ultimately to gain the victory'.

Kano studied ju-jutsu, principally from the Tenjin Shinyo Ryu and the Kito Ryu. In 1882 he began to teach his own method, known as Kodokan judo, a synthesis of the older ju-jutsu schools with Kano's own ideas derived from Western sports such as gymnastics. He regarded judo as more than a sport or fighting system: it was also intended to be a *do*, or spiritual way, followed only by those with the most developed moral sense, a gentleman's martial art. At the same time he rejected many of the old ideas, replacing the stress on *kan* (intuition) with rational thought and analysis. In this he was very much in tune with the wave of Western science and philosophy which swept Japan at the end of the nineteenth century.

Judo rapidly developed into a contest sport, becoming one of the events in the Olympics in 1964. In the eyes of many traditionalists it has lost more than it gained in this process. Training centres on developing competition skills, and all fighting is done in weight categories. Students first develop basic skills such as balance and the art of falling, moving on to learning various throws (*nage-waza* and *tachi-waza*) and groundwork (*ne-waza*). The third branch, known as the art of striking (*ate-waza*), has largely fallen into disuse in the West.

Aikido Created by Morihei Uyeshiba, the way of harmony is based on avoiding conflict by blending with an opponent's movements and neutralizing his attacks. The aikido master is said to resemble the eye of a hurricane, quiet in himself, but difficult to approach because of the tremendous forces swirling around him. Aikido is characterized by flowing circular movements and the use of vital energy, or *ki*. The techniques themselves were derived from Uyeshiba's study of many schools of ju-jutsu, spear fighting and sword arts. According to most historians, the greatest technical influence on aikido was the Daito Ryu, headed by Sokaku Takeda, a stern martial arts master who adhered rigidly to traditional values and beliefs. The theoretical side of aikido owes a great deal to the teachings of Bishop Deguchi and the Omotokyo sect, a curious religion rooted in nature worship and spirit possession. In fact, according to Uyeshiba, the true nature of the martial arts was revealed to him in a sudden flash of inspiration in 1925:

> As I was walking in the yard, the earth began shaking. Golden vapour gushed out of the earth enveloping my body, and I felt myself running into a golden body. I could understand what the chirping birds were saying and I understood clearly the creator's spirit. It was precisely at that moment that I received enlightenment: the fundamental principle of the martial arts is God's love and universal love. Tears of ecstasy rolled down my cheeks. . . . Martial training is not training that has as its primary purpose the defeating of others, but practice of God's love within ourselves.

With this end in view Uyeshiba opened a dojo in 1932, finally calling his system aikido in 1938. He rapidly gained a large following, including many who had studied judo and the classical arts of the sword and other weapons. After Uyeshiba'a death in 1969, many of his students created their own approach to aikido based largely on their beliefs and perceptions regarding fighting. Some groups make a determined effort to restructure the theoretical side of aikido to create an actual fighting system, while others regard it as a spiritual method, with little or nothing to do with fighting.

Weapons systems

The warrior class of Japan developed and made use of a wide range of weapons, including the bow and arrow, spear, halberd and sword. Of all the weapons taught, the sword was paramount; in fact Ieyasu Tokugawa, one of the great shoguns, said in his legacy: 'The sword is the soul of the samurai. If any should forget or lose it he will not be excused.'

The sword There are fundamentally three current approaches to training with the sword:

Kendo The way of the sword is practised widely in Japan. It is a system of sporting combat in which the participants wear armour and try to score points on designated targets with imitation bamboo swords (*shinai*). Many of its practitioners also regard it as a form of spiritual discipline and tend to disregard the sporting side.

Ken-jutsu This is the classical art of the Japanese sword. There are no sporting considerations in the training, which was created by master swordsmen with the sole aim of killing an enemy as quickly as possible. Training features the use of a real sword in kata practice and wooden weapons (*bokken*) in prearranged routines. The premier ken-jutsu school in Japan is the Tenshin Shoden Katori Shinto Ryu. One of the subsections of ken-jutsu is known as iai-jutsu, drawing the sword quickly and instantly dispatching an enemy with one or two techniques.

Iai-do This form of training emerged this century and is based on the technique of classical iai-jutsu, modified according to aesthetic considerations. There is little or no combat application of iai-do, as the method of sitting and wearing the sword ignores classical martial practices. There are many different schools of iai-do in Japan, but a type of standardized iai-do is taught by both the All Japan Kendo Federation and the All Japan Iai-do Federation.

Kyudo The way of the bow has a long and honourable history in Japan. The introduction of guns in the sixteenth century made the bow obsolete as a weapon of war, so changing its practice into a spiritual discipline in which hitting the target was not as important as the mental state of the archer. This is most strongly expressed in the most famous book on the system, *Zen in the Art of Archery* by E. Herrigel, written in the 1930s. Modern kyudo remains true to the concept of spiritual training, but is also involved to some extent in sporting competitions.

Naginata The *naginata* was originally a heavy type of halberd used by men on the battlefield. During the rule of the Tokugawa shoguns it was modified and used as a training weapon for samurai women, eventually evolving into a sport practised by women and featuring light bamboo weapons. The techniques featured in modern naginata-do bear little resemblance to the methods still taught by some of the traditional schools under the heading of naginata-jutsu. In 1953 an All Japan Naginata-do Federation was formed to promote a standardized system of training. Visitors to Japan can easily witness naginata training in the Butokuden in Kyoto.

Juken-do The way of the bayonet is a system which owes a great deal to Western influence. Organized as a sport in the 1950s, the techniques resemble those taught and practised in Britain at the end of the nineteenth century. The practitioner of juken-do wears protective armour and uses a wooden rifle and simulated bayonet, known as a *mokuju*. Points are scored by striking designated targets on an opponent in a competition. Training centres on developing strong thrusts.

Yari The spear is one of the oldest weapons known to man. In Japan it was used by samurai and warrior-priests (*so-hei*) to defend their land. Although obsolete by the seventeenth century, so-jutsu (the art of the spear) was preserved by the martial ryu and remained as one of the sources for the newer juken-do (bayonet fighting).

Jo The *jo* is a hardwood stick about 50 inches long and 1 inch in diameter. According to tradition, the founder of jo-jutsu was Muso Gonnosuke, a warrior who was never defeated until he fought the famous Miyamoto Musashi. Humiliated by his loss, he developed techniques using the *jo* with which he defeated Musashi. Jo-jutsu is built on twelve basic techniques which allow the practitioner to move in close to the opponent (always considered to be armed with a sword). Currently the *jo* is practised as a martial art (*jutsu*) and as a system of spiritual discipline (*do*). Training features kata practice and prearranged sparring drills.

Nin-jutsu The art of invisibility was developed by the *ninja*, professional military intelligence agents and assassins employed by the powerful Japanese clans in their long internal wars. The most famous ninja were from the Koga and Iga areas where they were trained from childhood in sabotage methods, combat skills and other arts necessary for their craft. They became expert in the use of conventional and unconventional weapons, including poison, bombs, primitive flame throwers and throwing knives.

At the moment nin-jutsu is going through a period of intense interest in the West. The best-known Japanese teacher is Masaaki Hatsumi, the teacher of Steven Hayes, one of the leading Western teachers of the art. Much of what passes for nin-jutsu is of very dubious origin, especially in the West, where many practitioners of karate, judo and aikido have created their own methods of nin-jutsu for commercial or other reasons. A great deal of the material available on nin-jutsu is not accurate and should be approached with great care.

Korea

As the natural land bridge between China and Japan, Korea was subjected to military and cultural invasions by both countries. The warriors of Korea developed martial arts both in response to invasion and for civil war. The political unification of Korea in the tenth century and the diplomatic relationship with China influenced the development of Korean fighting systems, as did the Mongol invasions in the thirteenth century. During the Yi dynasty (1392–1910) martial arts were despised and ignored, leading to a loss of technical skill and the virtual extinction of many methods. In this century the Japanese systems of judo, kendo and ju-jutsu were introduced and practised widely, leading to a rebirth of interest in the traditional Korean arts.

Kicking and punching systems

Taekwondo Due to lack of official interest in the martial arts, many of the traditional systems barely survived. After the Second World War there was a deliberate attempt by a number of individuals and organizations to create a new Korean martial art. By combining Okinawan and Japanese karate systems with the surviving elements of native Korean methods, a new system gradually emerged which became known as taekwondo. The name is derived from: *tae* (to kick), *kwon* (to punch) and *do* (the way or method), and so may be translated as 'the way of kicking and punching'. The name, accepted at a meeting of the leading teachers in 1955, was created by General Choi Hong Hi, the man known as the father of taekwondo. Although most Korean teachers state that taekwondo was developed from older Korean and Chinese systems, it is in fact obvious that the system was based largely on Japanese karate, even using the same kata in the 1950s and 1960s. Taekwondo is now developing along its own lines, stressing jumping kicks, the ability to break stones, tiles and wooden boards, and the development of specific taekwondo *hyung* (kata or sets). Due to its initial development and organization, taekwondo has gained Olympic recognition.

Hapkido This system is similar to taekwondo in some respects in that it uses a wide range of kicking techniques. However, it also makes use of a wide range of throwing and locking movements not usually seen in taekwondo. It was founded by Yung Shul Choi, a student of Daito Ryu aiki-jutsu, who trained in Japan from 1919 until the 1930s. He combined his knowledge of Japanese ju-jutsu with Korean methods to create hapkido in the late 1950s. Because of its connection with Daito Ryu aiki-jutsu, many of the throwing techniques resemble those taught by aikido teachers.

There are many systems derived from these two methods, as well as modifications of Chinese or Japanese systems. Usually they claim descent from the *hwarang do,* a Korean version of the Japanese samurai, but in fact most of the methods taught in Korea are no more than fifty years old and often owe more to their creator's imagination than any true historical derivation.

Grappling systems

Yudo This is the Korean version of Kodokan judo. The Korean Yudo Association was formed in September 1945 in Seoul, to promote a specifically Korean approach to judo. Technically there is little difference between the Korean and Japanese approaches to judo and in fact the Korean judo team enters the world judo championships in Tokyo.

Cireum This is a general term for all systems of wrestling practised in Korea. Basically a system deriving from Chinese shuai-chiao allied to typical peasant grappling methods, the wrestlers wear a loincloth and try to throw one another to the ground. Choking, striking and ground fighting are not permitted. In many ways it resembles Cumberland and Westmorland wrestling found in the north of England.

Weapons systems

Archery Historically the Koreans were famous for their skills in both mounted and unmounted archery. These skills were developed in response to the threats of invasion by powerful neighbours to the north and south (China and Japan); a large enemy force could be destroyed by a numerically inferior force of archers, as the English did to the French at Agincourt. The Korean Archery Association was established in 1922 to organize archery demonstrations and competitions and to preserve the distinctly Korean style as a modern sport.

The sword The Korean Kumdo (Kendo) Association was founded in 1948 to promote and regulate the practice of Japanese kendo in Korea. Technically it is the same as the Japanese style.

Various martial schools teach the use of the sword and knife. Generally speaking, the use of the weapons is dictated largely by empty-hand methods.

Thailand and Burma

Thailand and Burma, situated as they are between the great mother cultures of Asia, India and China, have long been influenced by both. All the fighting systems developed by the Thais and Burmese bear witness to this, but the Thais and Burmese have added their own specific talents to produce systems of tremendous efficiency. Between 1551, when the state of Burma was created from the people of Indo-China, to 1885, when the British took over, Thailand and Burma were in a state of almost continuous war. In fact, at times Thailand was successfully invaded and occupied by the Burmese. This has led to a great deal of interdependence in the development of martial skills, as any gain by one side has to be copied or improved on by the other. It has led to the situation in which the martial arts of both countries are very similar in technical content, training methods, etc. This is generally true of the whole area; Cambodia and Laos also are home to systems very similar to those practised in Thailand and Burma.

Thailand

Kicking and punching systems

Thai boxing (muay thai) One of the most devastating fighting systems in the world, Thai boxing uses the full range of natural weapons to defeat an opponent. The modern version has been influenced by Western boxing to some extent, improving the punching and defensive skills of the fighters, but the knee, elbow and shin techniques are derived from the traditional art.

In the past muay thai was practised by warriors as part of their martial training. According to tradition, Yi Kumkam became king of Thailand in the fifteenth century by defeating his brother Fang Ken in a boxing match. This method was chosen to avoid the bloodshed of a civil war which could have destroyed the country. Before the adoption of boxing gloves, Thai boxers covered their fists with leather thongs or hemp rope. It is said that ground glass was glued to the rope to make the punching more effective! By the 1930s boxing gloves were adopted.

Technically Thai boxers are considered to be skilled in the use of the leg, knee and elbow, but, compared to Western boxers, they are poor punchers. Grappling is not permitted in the ring and, of course, there is no ground fighting. In matches against French boxers and Chinese kung-fu fighters the Thai fighters usually win. This is probably due to the intensity of their training and the sheer fighting spirit they develop rather than to any technical superiority. Training is very similar to that followed by Western boxers, with the addition of special methods to develop kicking power. The Thais make great use of the shin, using it to strike an opponent's head, body or supporting leg; a common tactic is to destroy an opponent's mobility by kicking his thighs and lower legs, then move in with the knee, elbow and fists to finish the match. Some idea of the ferocity of the action may be obtained from the following account published in the *Bangkok Sunday Post* in 1965:

> The contestants size each other up for a moment and then let loose with a series of punches, kicks and elbow jolts that make the tourists wonder – is this sport?
>
> But sport it is and as the card progresses they start to pick up the rules and see the skill demanded.
>
> An over-keen fighter swings his chunky leg at an opponent and then feels his own legs and body pummelled as he swings around off balance. Sometimes the fighters battle themselves to a standstill after the five three minute rounds and hang on the ropes gasping for air while the decision is made. Sometimes they lose by a technical knockout when they can't continue because of injury. Sometimes a boxer finishes the bout sprawled unconscious on the canvas – this is what the crowd came for and the cheers are deafening.

Sila In the southern provinces of Pattani, Yala and Naruthiwat, the people practise a folk dance/fighting system known as *sila*. The practitioners wear Malay-style clothing and perform to music, usually spending ten minutes or so to complete the 'dance'. Actually sila is a Thai adaption of the Indonesian fighting system known as *silat*. It was taken to Thailand by Malay merchants from Menangkabau, an area of Sumatra famous for the ferocity of its warriors. There is no doubt that, although disguised as a folk dance, sila remains a very effective method of self-defence.

Grappling systems

Methods of wrestling have never been very popular among the Thais, probably due to their relatively slim physiques. Japanese judo has some following, but the technical standard is not high. It is said that various types of wrestling are practised among the hill tribes, but not much is known about the systems practised.

Weapon systems

Krabee krabong Krabee krabong (sword and staff), also known as fan dab, is the Thai system of fighting with sword, staff, knife and other weapons. Thai swords are often used in pairs and are matched against other swords, staffs or clubs. Training is usually performed as prearranged two-man drills, but because of the speed and power of the fighters injuries are by no means unknown. As well as the systems taught by the Thais, other methods are practised by the hill tribes who live in the north of Thailand. It is likely that both the Thai style and methods taught by the hill tribes have been influenced by Chinese models. Krabee krabong was always associated with the Thai royal family. King Chulalongkorn used to perform a sword drill while seated on the neck of a war elephant as a tribute to the Buddha.

Although krabee krabong went through something of a decline, it is growing in popularity again. This is due to the efforts of a number of people, one of the most important being

Mr Samai Mesamarna, the master of the Buddhai Sawan, the fencing school of Thailand. His leading students now teach the art in universities, private schools, etc. According to Acharn (Master) Samai, 'a good fighter moves his weapons so rapidly around his body that his opponent cannot see his weak point and cannot get a clear thrust. This rapid movement must be done automatically, as one's concentration must be on seeking out the vulnerable part of the opponent's defence and then striking there.'

All Thai fighting systems use music in training and in fighting to develop the fighters' speed and rhythm; because of this many uninformed observers regard some of the training as dancing. Nothing could be farther from the truth.

Burma

All Burmese systems of fighting may be grouped under the general title of *thaing* or self-defence. In the 1930s this expression was used to cover all the systems taught in Burma, but nowadays there is a tendency to refer to different systems by more specific titles. During the Second World War, Burmese systems were exposed to many Japanese systems and were reorganized, taking much from aikido, judo and ju-jutsu in the process.

Kicking and punching systems

Burmese boxing (bama letwhay) Basically there is little or no difference between Thai and Burmese boxing, although the Burmese tend to be heavier on average and therefore slightly more powerful. However, whereas Thai boxing is a professional sport in Thailand, Burmese boxing is not as organized and lacks the professional element. It is also true to say that due to the influence of Western boxing on the Thai style, Burmese boxing is not as technically developed.

In America Dr Maung Gyi has formed the American Bando Association which organizes, teaches and promotes Burmese boxing. Technically Maung Gyi's bando has been influenced by Western boxing training methods, using gloves, sparring equipment and heavy bags to develop skills, rather than the bare-knuckle form of fighting originally practised in Burma. This approach follows that of his father, Li Ba Than, a Burmese master who began to modernize and reform the older systems in the late 1940s. Modern bando is a fusion of Burmese boxing, traditional bando (a softer, more elusive system than bama letwhay) and Western boxing.

Grappling systems

Wrestling (naban) Burmese wrestling is relatively undeveloped, lacking the technical sophistication of judo or Indian methods. Practised mainly by the mountain tribes, the Chins and the Kachins, it enjoys some following in the cities.

Weapons systems

The general term for all weapons use is *banshay*. There are systems which teach the use of the sword, spear and staff. As in Japanese martial arts, the sword is the central weapon. The Burmese sword is identical in type and use to the Thai weapon. Training consists of practising sets and prearranged sparring routines. According to U. Pye Thein in his work, *Burmese Fencing*:

> The Burmese sword is not particularly meant for thrusts. It is specially meant for slashing left and right with a view to disabling or disarming an assailant.
>
> The need to wield two swords simultaneously necessitates the use of both feet in executing footwork, which looks quite complicated to an uninitiated person. To make the techniques of attack and defence effective, practice has to be made on various methods of footwork and fundamentals of attack and defence.

Indonesia and Malaysia

The arts and cultures found in this area show influences derived from many sources. The cultures of China, India, Indo-China, Arabia and Europe have all contributed to the martial methods found in Indonesia and Malaysia. Many of the inhabitants were fishermen and traders, often journeying long distances in the course of their work. Typical of these were the Bugis, a people famous as adventurers, merchants and mercenaries. Their martial skills were noted by a Chinese writer, Wang Ta-hae, in 1783:

In foreign countries to the south west, all the people learn military exercises. The Bugis, in particular, admire bravery and when their skill in the use of weapons is great, they are praised by their parents, and respected by their townsmen, being honoured with the title of gustee. . . . Throughout the whole region, everyone submits to those who are skilled in military tactics; hence both men and women, from their tenth year upwards, accustom themselves to the use of the sword and spear, and are acquainted with the method of jumping and springing on the foe. . . . I once had a slave girl called Chang Choo who accompanied me to Benjarmasin. On the way we were attacked by pirates; I was much alarmed and lost command of myself. The crew of the vessel also said, 'Few against many, what can we do?' The slave girl said, 'Since it has come to this we must exert our strength.' However I did not know what to do, when the girl cried out, 'Never fear' and grasping a spear she went forth and mounted guard at the companion-way without moving. When the thieves came on board, they rushed aft, but the maid brandishing her spear wounded several of them. The pirates fell back and said to each other, 'How is it that she has got the Buginese method of spear fighting?' On which the slave girl shouted out, 'I also am a Buginese: come and let us have another round!' The thieves were however alarmed and retreated in confusion.

Wang Ta-hae also recounts a case in which a Chinese merchant named Te Hao was attacked by Javanese pirates while on a trip to Banda. His servants, who were Bugis, defeated the pirates, who were forced to apologize and pay compensation for attacking the ship!

Kicking and punching systems

Pentjak-silat This is a general term used to describe Indonesian empty-hand fighting systems. The Malay equivalent is known as bersilat. Technically, the expression covers a tremendous variety of systems and methods, some stressing low stances with wide, expansive movements such as the Hariman or tiger style found in Sumatra, while others favour more upright stances such as those found in the Javanese style known as perisai diri. According to some authorities, there are over 150 styles of pentjak-silat, most of which are to be found on Java. It is obvious that some of these styles have been influenced by modern (i.e. post-1945) Japanese karate, as they have distinctive Japanese features including a belt system and use kicking methods such as the side-thrust kick and roundhouse kick performed in the distinctive Japanese way.

Kuntao A Chinese expression meaning 'fist way', kuntao is used to describe all the Chinese systems of combat practised in Indonesia and Malaysia. Traditionally kept secret, these systems were practised by the Chinese communities found throughout Indonesia. Systems include Fukien White Crane boxing, Tai-chi-ch'uan, Lohan boxing and various systems from Shantung.

Grappling systems

Most styles of pentjak-silat include techniques of grappling, throwing and locking. As well as these methods, there are two systems in which grappling and throwing techniques predominate:

Gulat A style of wrestling found in Java, gulat is a fusion of Korean cireum, Japanese sumo and Iranian/Western freestyle wrestling. This synthesis came about due to the Japanese control of the area during the Second World War.

Okol Found on Madura Island, okol is a form of wrestling in which victory is obtained by throwing an opponent to the ground; no ground fighting is permitted.

Weapons systems

The range of weapons taught and practised in Indonesia and Malaysia is almost limitless. All the styles of pentjak-silat and kuntao teach the use of weapons, which include sticks of various lengths, swords, spears, knives, chains, whips, blow-pipes, bows and arrows and a variety of composite weapons. Perhaps the best known of the wide range of weapons available is the *kris*, a double-edged dagger used for thrusting. The blade is sometimes straight, but is often made with a series of undulations, said to help in penetrating an opponent's body. Another weapon utilized by many pentjak-silat styles is the *tjebang*, a weapon which is identical to the Okinawan *sai*. It is likely that both the *tjebang* and the *sai* evolved from South Chinese originals.

The Philippines

Up to a few years ago Filipino martial arts were relatively unknown in the West. However, they are now being seriously studied in many Western countries as they have proved to be very effective. The people of the Philippines developed various systems in response to foreign invasion and internal warfare. The Philippine islands have been invaded and occupied by Indians, Chinese, Spaniards, Americans and Japanese. From all these invaders the Filipinos absorbed martial techniques, so improving their own methods. The Moslem Filipinos, known as the Moros, exemplify the proud martial tradition which eventually developed. It is said that American soldiers had to be equipped with ·45-calibre pistols, as the Moro warriors could not be stopped with ·38s!

Kicking and punching systems

Sikaran Found mainly on the island of Luzon, sikaran is a system of fighting which stresses kicks and leg techniques, although the hands are used in defence. The techniques resemble karate and taekwondo to a large extent and have been absorbed by most karate systems in the Philippines. It is unlikely that sikaran can survive in a pure form as it cannot compete with karate in terms of organization and promotion. However, it is likely that it will influence the development of a distinctive Filipino karate style.

Grappling systems

Some judo and wrestling is practised in the Philippines, but grappling systems as such have never been very popular.

Weapons systems

It is in the use of weapons that the Filipino martial tradition really excels. The favourite weapons are knives, sticks, spears and *bolos*, a heavy machete-like weapon. The earliest name for this art was *kali*, a system which made use of knives and sticks. During the Spanish occupation kali was banned, so forcing it to be practised in secret. The Filipinos blended the art of kali with techniques taken from Spanish swordplay, so producing a method known as *arnis de mano* or *escrima*. To avoid suspicion, training in this system was set to music and performed as a dance, but the Spanish rulers often discovered the deadliness of the method when rebellions broke out against their rule – a common feature of Filipino history.

There are many schools of escrima, but they share some common points. In general a student learns to fight with a stick, moving on to two sticks as skill increases. The same techniques can be performed with bladed weapons, both long and short, and eventually with empty hands. Unlike most systems, a student of escrima begins with weapons and progresses to the empty hand. Training features the practice of basic strikes and blocks in thin air and with a partner; some modern instructors have included judo throws and sweeps to widen their technical repertoire. In the past challenge fights were quite common, often featuring knives and *bolos*, but the purists prefer the sticks, as they believe a stick in skilled hands can be more effective than a knife. There is a modern trend to develop escrima as a sport, in which points would be scored against an armoured opponent. This is fiercely resisted by the older masters who fear it will weaken the traditional art.

The West

The history of Europe and America could never be described as peaceful. The long internecine wars in Europe that have occurred since the fall of the Roman Empire, together with the frequent civil wars and wars caused by imperial ambitions, led to the development of weapons and fighting techniques equal to anything found in the Orient. The popularity of duelling among the upper class led to an intensive development of sword fighting, and so to the creation of various styles of swordsmanship. Among the lower class, fists, sticks and knives were often used to settle arguments or disagreements, and a man who could not or would not fight was despised as a coward or weakling. The development of firearms led to the abandonment of most of these methods, as pragmatic Westerners could not see any value in retaining obsolete systems. Fortunately some were modified and preserved as combat sports.

Kicking and punching systems

Boxing First organized by the Greeks and Romans, the boxers of classical Greece and Rome fought in the arena, often to the death. They wore gloves and hand wrappings of cloth or leather to protect their fists, but under Roman influence boxers began to use the *myrmax* or loaded *cestus* (glove), a stone or metal weapon which meant that all blows were potentially lethal. The classical Greek approach, which was to regard boxing as an athletic pastime rather than a fight to the death, survived until the 291st Olympiad (AD 393), although the Romans regarded the Greek style as weak and effeminate due to the absence of loaded gloves.

In the eighteenth century, boxing was reborn in England. Men such as James Figg and Jack Broughton began to organize and demonstrate the 'noble art of self-defence'. In 1743 the first set of rules regulating boxing was published and the first champions emerged. The fighting included punching and throwing; one valued technique was to close on to an opponent and throw him with a 'cross-buttock', landing on him heavily. As the boxers all fought with bare knuckles the matches featured a good deal of blood and facial injuries; in fact, if the 'claret' did not flow the spectators would often riot and end the fight! The fights, although illegal, were often patronized by the upper class; in fact, it was quite common for sons of the nobility to take lessons in boxing from the champions of the day. Technical innovations and improvements were made by boxers such as Tom Cribb, Daniel Mendoza and 'Gentleman' John Jackson, who was considered to be the British and world heavyweight champion in 1789. Daniel Mendoza, who lost the championship to Jackson, left a record of his thoughts and observations on boxing:

> The first principle in boxing to be established is to be perfectly master of the equilibrium of the body, so as to be able to change from a right to a left handed position, to advance or retreat, striking or parrying, and to throw the body backward or forward, without difficulty or embarrassment.
>
> The second principle to be established is the position of the body, which should be in an inclining posture or diagonal line, so as to place the pit of the stomach out of your adversary's reach: both knees must be bent, the left leg advanced, and the arms directly before your throat or chin.
>
> It should be an invariable rule to stop or parry your adversary's right with your left, and his left with your right; and, both in striking and parrying, always to keep your stomach guarded, by barring it with your left or right fore arm. . . .
>
> If your adversary aims round blows (the case of a man ignorant of boxing), you should strike forward, as a direct line reaches its object sooner than one that is circular.

The bare-knuckle era came to an end with John L. Sullivan, the famous 'Boston Strong Boy'. His defeat by James J. Corbett ushered in the modern style of boxing which features padded gloves and the Marquis of Queensberry rules. Sullivan himself welcomed this, for he wrote:

> The London rules allow too much leeway for the rowdy element to indulge in their practices. Such mean tricks as spiking, biting, gouging, concealing snuff in one's mouth to blind an opponent, strangling, butting with the head, falling down without being struck, scratching with the nails, kicking, falling on an antagonist with the knees, the using of stones and resin, are impossible under the Queensberry Rules. Fighting under the new rules before gentlemen is a pleasure.

Nowadays boxing is practised as an amateur and as a professional sport. All boxers are subject to strict medical checks and all fights are carefully controlled. Training features bag punching, skipping, running and sparring. It is probably true to say that, of all the current fighting systems, boxing is one of the best regulated and organized. The boxers themselves are also among the best-conditioned fighters in the world.

Savate and French boxing Savate was created in France in the eighteenth century. The system concentrated on using low kicks to an opponent's knees, shins and groin, as well as some grappling techniques. It was employed mainly by the criminal elements in Paris, while a related system known as *chausson* was followed by soldiers in the South of France. According to Alexandre Dumas, a leading teacher of savate named Charles Lecour created French boxing by combining savate with English boxing. He studied under two London fighters, Adams and Smith, creating French boxing in 1852. Within ten years, Lecour's students became famous for their fighting skills, one of the most important being J. Charlemont, an excellent boxer in his own right and an inspired teacher. Soon the art was adopted by the upper class, who regarded it as a valuable method of self-defence. A system of stick fighting based on fencing techniques was created. Known as *canne,* it was taught alongside the kicking and punching methods. In 1898, a book in English was written by Georges D'Amoric, which illustrated the complete system. Comparing it with contemporary Chinese and Okinawan methods, it is interesting to note that French boxing was technically far in advance of anything found in the oriental systems. The French method included side kicks, high roundhouse kicks, back kicks and sweeping and throwing techniques. According to Henry Williams in an article in *Physical Culture* published in August 1900:

> The professors of the art practise all day long kicking at imaginary things. Their accuracy is remarkable. With a side kick as high as the head they can knock the ashes off a cigar without injuring the fire. They never seem to lose their equilibrium, and always land with the weight on the rear foot, with the front foot swinging and ready for immediate action.

The carnage of the First World War and the subsequent economic problems in Europe left French boxing shattered. Only a few individuals preserved the art, but nowadays it is again growing in popularity, ironically enough because of the interest originally generated by oriental arts.

Capoeira The most unusual martial art in the West, capoeira developed in Brazil in the eighteenth and nineteenth centuries. Its roots lie in the dances and fighting systems brought to Brazil by African slaves. They produced a method, characterized by acrobatic kicks and strikes, which features avoiding an opponent's blows rather than simply blocking them. As well as developing empty-hand skills, capoeiristas also adapted knives, razors, bottles, sticks and swords to their system. Capoeira was practised mainly by the lower class and was identified in the official mind with criminals and other antisocial elements. For many years it was banned, so the teachers and students practised it as a dance. For this reason, music is still an important element in training, the sound of the *berimban* (a stringed instrument) marking a capoeira training session.

Capoeira has managed to shake off its reputation for violence and is now accepted by the Brazilian government as an art form and an official sport. The techniques have been analysed carefully and organized into a logical sequence to aid in instruction, and various organizations have emerged, some of them outside Brazil. In 1980 the World Capoeira Association was founded in California by Bira Almeida, a student of one of the greatest teachers of the art, Mestre (Master) Bimba. Public demonstrations have been held with some success and interest in the art is growing.

Grappling systems

Wrestling has a long history in the West. The Greeks and Romans encouraged it as part of military training and included it in the Olympic and other games. Two types or styles of wrestling were developed:

(a) standing wrestling, in which victory was decided by throwing an opponent to the ground;

(b) the *pankration*, which was a form of all-out fighting using throws, kicks, punches and locks.

In the Middle Ages, all European countries practised wrestling of one type or another. In 1443, Talhofer wrote a book on combat methods, the *Fechtbuch* (*Book on Fighting*), which showed grappling methods very similar to those used today. In Britain regional styles abounded, perhaps the best known being the

Cornish, the Lancashire and the Cumberland and Westmorland. Wrestling was not simply practised by commoners. Milton states in his work *On Education* that wrestling should be part of the education of a gentleman.

Many of these methods were taken to America by the early colonists, where they influenced the development of the 'catch-as-catch-can' style of wrestling. Abraham Lincoln was said to be one of the best wrestlers of this style in southern Illinois. The two most popular styles of wrestling nowadays are:

(a) Graeco-Roman, which concentrates mainly on standing wrestling, although some ground fighting is permitted;

(b) Freestyle wrestling, which includes all the techniques of standing wrestling, plus a wide range of techniques for fighting on the ground.

Both styles of wrestling are practised, but freestyle wrestling is probably the most popular, especially in America and Russia. One Russian variation on freestyle wrestling is sambo, which combines judo and wrestling techniques. This style is spreading through the West and is gaining popularity in both the judo and wrestling worlds.

Weapons systems

The types and range of weapons produced in the West since Roman times are unmatched by any other culture, except possibly by the Chinese. From the fall of the Roman Empire to the evolution of the gun, warriors of all the nations of Europe developed various weapons and styles of using them. The Vikings favoured the long sword and the axe, while the knights of the Middle Ages were expected to be skilful in the use of the sword, spear, war hammer and mace. A class of professional teachers emerged, some of whom wrote technical manuals (often known as *Fechtbücher*) to record their techniques and training methods. Armour developed from simple chain mail to complex arrangements of plate armour. This caused an evolution in the design and use of the sword; large two-handed swords intended to smash through the armour were made, as were longer thinner-bladed weapons designed to thrust through the gaps where the plates overlapped. The latter eventually evolved into the rapier. Simpler weapons were not neglected, and the English in particular were famous for their use of the staff. In 1625 an Englishman armed with a staff defeated three Spanish fighters armed with rapiers and daggers. English masters of defence such as George Silver kept alive the traditions of the older methods of fighting, maintaining them against the elaborate and complex methods developed in France, Italy and Spain.

Certainly skill with the staff and single stick was kept alive until the beginning of the twentieth century. In 1903 *Self-Defence* was written by R. G. Allanson-Winn and C. E. Walker. In this work, methods of fighting using the staff, single stick and walking stick are shown. It is interesting to compare them with oriental methods. They are in no way technically inferior to any oriental system. Unfortunately there is no one teaching these methods as the last instructors died in the early years of this century. However, sufficient published material remains to resurrect the old European schools; perhaps in the future this may happen.

3 Karate: History and Styles

History of Karate

China

Although the history of karate is difficult to trace, it is quite certain that karate-like methods were taught and practised in China many centuries ago. Indeed, there are scattered references to 'dances' being used as preparation for battle (666 BC), boxers who could kill wild animals and smash stones with their fists (1000 BC) and competitions which featured kicking and punching techniques (AD 100). In general these methods were developed by soldiers for use in battle. An early reference to empty-hand fighting is to be found in the literature of the Spring and Autumn period (722–481 BC). In 681 BC the armies of the states of Chin and Ch'u stood waiting to fight. The commander of the Chin army, the Marquis of Chin, dreamed that he was boxing with the enemy commander, the Viscount of Ch'u, who knocked him down and knelt down to suck out his brains! Naturally, he regarded this as a bad omen, but his chief adviser optimistically pointed out that he was on his back looking up to heaven, while the viscount was kneeling as if in admission of wrongdoing. In the ensuing battle the Chin army totally destroyed the army of Ch'u.

The Chinese fighting arts gradually evolved, absorbing concepts from oriental medical and religious beliefs. There is no doubt that the Shaolin Temple in Honan Province was an important centre of technical development, especially in staff methods. Many legends surround the Shaolin, most of which have entered the popular history of the martial arts. However, there is no evidence that Bodhidharma taught anything other than meditation to the monks, and as for the books he is said to have written, the Muscle Change Classic (I Chin Ching) and the Marrow Washing Classic (Hsi Sui Ching), they are known to be products of the nineteenth century.

As the power and wealth of China increased, the surrounding nations came to be more and more influenced by Chinese culture and philosophy. Many nations, including Japan, Korea, Cambodia, Laos and Thailand, deliberately copied Chinese education, pottery, philosophy, social organization, medicine, town planning, religion and military systems. In many cases they ceased to be independent states, but were simply Chinese vassal states, whose rulers owed allegiance to the Chinese emperors. Because of this, diplomatic and trade missions often moved between China and her cultural vassals, so spreading Chinese fighting methods to other countries. Foreign students came to China to study a wide variety of subjects; for example, it is known that a Japanese monk, Shoogen (1296–1364), was a student at the Shaolin Temple for twenty-one years and was highly respected by all who met him.

By the end of the nineteenth century a multitude of styles had evolved. The basic division of hard or external systems and soft or internal systems had evolved, along with an extensive theoretical background drawn from Taoism and Buddhism, dealing with breathing, power, striking points and movement, etc. All of this affected the development of karate.

Okinawa

While it is possible to see karate-like systems in China, the formulation and development of karate as a distinct art owes more to Okinawa than China. It is probably true to say that karate resulted from a fusion of Chinese methods mainly from Fukien with an indigenous Okinawan system known as *te*, or hand. The theoretical and philosophical aspects were most certainly derived from Chinese roots, as Okinawa was a cultural backwater with no native literature or philosophy to speak of beyond peasant folklore and nature religion.

In 1372 the king of Okinawa, Satsudo, became a vassal of the Ming dynasty and the Chinese began to send imperial envoys to Okinawa. Between 1372 and 1806, twenty-three envoys visited Okinawa, along with hundreds of soldiers, clerks, scholars and artisans. They usually stayed in Kumemura village for six months or so before returning to China. In 1392 thirty-six families of Chinese artisans arrived in Okinawa as settlers. Through these contacts Chinese martial arts and culture were introduced to the Okinawan people.

The development of empty-hand methods and the use of simple weapons was stimulated by the decrees in the sixteenth and seventeenth centuries against the use of swords and other weapons. It is said that the adaptation of farming and fishing tools to fighting methods began at this time, although there is no real proof of this. In the eighteenth, nineteenth and twentieth centuries it is recorded that a number of Okinawans went to China to study martial arts and, at the same time, Chinese methods were displayed openly in Okinawa. Although information is often scarce, the following facts are reliable:

In 1762 a Chinese known as Kung Hsiang-chun demonstrated fighting methods in Okinawa.

'Karate' Sakugawa (1733–1815), who lived in Shuri city, studied karate under Takahara and Chinese systems from Kung Hsiang-chun.

1762: the *Oshima Hikki* by Tobe Yoshihiro was published. It refers to Chinese kempo and the kata wanshu.

Sokon 'Bushi' Matsumura (1798–1890), a great karate master and student of Sakugawa, is said to have fought and defeated a bull.

Yasutsune Itosu (1830–1914) became in 1846 a student of Matsumura. In time he became recognized as a karate *meijin*, or genius. He developed the five Pinan kata, Bassai-sho and Kanku-sho.

In 1877 Kanryo Higaonna (1853–1915) went to Fukien Province, where he studied Chinese boxing under Liu Liang-hsing. He returned to Okinawa and began teaching his system in Naha in 1885. He modified the Chinese methods to suit the Okinawan physique. The essence of his system was the practice of Sanchin kata.

Gichin Funakoshi (1868–1957), a student of Itosu and Azato, along with

Choki Motobu introduced karate into Japan in 1922. His teaching formed the base for the development of the Shotokan style.

In 1897 Kanbun Uechi (1877–1948) went to Fukien Province, where he studied Chinese boxing under Chou Tze-ho (1874–1926), a leading teacher of Fukien boxing. Chou Tze-ho was highly skilled in Tiger boxing (Hu Ch'uan), the influence of which can still be seen in the katas of Uechi Ryu, the style of karate created by Kanbun Uechi and currently headed by his son, Kanei Uechi.

In 1902 Chojun Miyagi (1888–1953) began to study Naha-te karate under Kanryo Higaonna. On his teacher's death in 1915 he visited China, returning for subsequent visits in 1917 and 1936. The style he created, Goju Ryu, is now one of the leading systems in Okinawa.

Kenwa Mabuni (1893–1957) a student of Itosu and Higaonna, created Shito Ryu karate. In 1929 he moved to Osaka, taking his method to Japan where it rapidly became one of the major schools.

By the beginning of this century Okinawan karate was well developed with many skilled teachers and students. It entered the school system as a form of physical training, so spreading its teachings to a wider and more educated following. In 1921 karate was demonstrated to the future emperor of Japan, Hirohito, who was very impressed with what he saw. This led in turn to the spread of karate to the Japanese mainland.

Traditional Okinawan karate was never considered a sport. Its purpose was to develop powerful techniques to kill or injure an opponent. In 1872, Okinawan karate skills were observed by Ernest Satow, who wrote:

As regards more manly accomplishments, they are expert archers on horseback and good marksmen with the matchlock. Their skill in boxing is such that a well trained fighter can smash a large earthen water-jar, or kill a man with a single blow of his fist.

Seiji Noma, the founder of Kodansha, the publishers, lived on Okinawa at the beginning of the century. He comments:

The Luchuans had developed through centuries the practice of the peculiar art of self-defence and aggression known as *tekobushi*, which consists in making incredibly deft and powerful thrusts of the fist after the fashion of jujitsu or even boxing. . . . A Luchuan expert in this deadly art could smash every bone in his victim's body with the thrusts of his arms, as if he had struck with a giant hammer. Not infrequently poor victims were found dead by the road-side bearing marks of terrible blows from naked fists. Near Tsuji at night there were always gangs of roughs supposed to be skilled in *tekobushi,* who were ready to pick quarrels with unwary strangers.

Okinawan karate can be classified into two groups: Naha-te, which includes Goju Ryu and Uechi Ryu, and Shuri-te, which includes all the Shorin Ryu groups. Chinese influence can be most easily seen on the Naha-te systems, the kata, breathing methods and general training methods resembling systems from South China. There seems to be a process of 'Okinawaization' of Chinese methods, which involves adding the use of the *chi-ishi* (strength stone), *kame* (jar) and *makiwara* (punching post) to Chinese-derived techniques. This seems to be happening to Uechi Ryu at the moment, so leading it farther away from its Chinese origins.

Japan

In 1921, the Crown Prince, Hirohito, visited Okinawa and saw a karate demonstration by Miyagi, Shinko Matayoshi and some schoolchildren. The demonstration was arranged by Gichin Funakoshi, then head of the Shobukai, an Okinawan karate group. Inspired by this success, Funakoshi arrived in Tokyo in June 1922, where he demonstrated karate at a sports exhibition and at the headquarters of judo, the Kodokan.

This new martial art was so well received that Funakoshi stayed in Tokyo, teaching karate to groups of soldiers, police, students and other martial artists. Other instructors arrived from Okinawa, the most important being Choki Motobu and Kenwa Mabuni, and within a few years karate dojos could be found all over Japan. In 1924 Keio University opened a karate dojo; by 1937 ten universities had karate dojos teaching a variety of styles. Funakoshi's top student, Hironori Otsuka, formed his own style of karate, Wado Ryu (way of harmony), by blending ju-jutsu techniques and concepts with the Okinawan karate taught to him by Funakoshi and Mabuni. The creation of Wado Ryu marked the emergence of a distinctive Japanese approach to the art. Inspired by the examples of judo and kendo, grading systems were adopted, the first black belts being awarded by Funakoshi in April 1924 to Tokuda, Otsuka, Akiba, Shimizu, Hirose, Gima and Kasuya. Groups unconnected with Funakoshi followed his lead and the distinctive dan/kyu system was adopted. In the 1930s experiments with sparring methods led to a movement away from the importance of kata and the emergence of competitive sparring.

The use of free-style sparring, unknown in Okinawa, led to the development of new techniques. It is said that Yoshitaka (Giko) Funakoshi (Funakoshi's son) was responsible for developing the side-thrust kick and the roundhouse kick, although this is probably overstating the case to some extent. However, it is true to say that by the 1940s and 1950s Japanese karate was developing in a way quite different from that of Okinawa.

In fact, the Japanese asserted their independence from Okinawan values and beliefs in the 1930s. In 1936 the Japanese began to write karate with the characters which read 'empty hand' instead of the Okinawan use of the characters for 'China hand'. Gichin Funakoshi also changed the Okinawan and Chinese names of the kata to Japanese names in order to make karate more acceptable to a more sophisticated Japanese public. It is noticeable that Funakoshi wanted to spread karate among the more educated Japanese and so anything which identified karate as a provincial peasant art was avoided. In 1935 the Dai Nippon Butokukai (Great Japan Martial Arts Association) awarded the rank of *renshi* to Miyagi, Ueshima and Konishi, and in 1938 the same rank was awarded to Funakoshi, Otsuka, Mabuni and others. To the traditional Okinawan masters this lessened the prestige of the title, as Konishi, Funakoshi's student, was on the board which awarded the grade to Funakoshi!

After the war the major groups began to organize into large associations, based on the example given by judo. Stress was placed on developing competition skills and the katas were changed to make them more aesthetically pleasing. It was realized by the leaders of Japanese karate that tournaments and a sporting approach would be the best way to spread karate to the West, and so most of the styles made this their ideal; indeed, some systems were created solely for competition use. The leaders of these groups still paid lipservice to the classical Okinawan ideals, but in fact their karate was quite different in appearance and intent to that of Okinawa. Japanese karate was linear and the techniques were intended to be used against another karate-ka in a competitive situation, whereas Okinawan karate featured more curved movements and was intended to be used against an untrained attacker in self-defence.

In 1962 the Federation of All Japan Karate Organizations (FAJKO) was founded. A set of competition rules was published, judges and referees were trained and inter-style competitions were arranged.

Many Japanese methods are now almost totally involved in competition-based karate. For many people skill is defined as tournament ability and the katas have been so modified that they can only teach self-defence techniques in the most contrived of situations. For this reason some Japanese karate-ka are now looking at the older Okinawan methods as bases to re-examine their own systems, in order to reintroduce the ideal of effective self-defence. Possibly this is due to the fact that Japan no longer dominates the competitive aspect of karate and is simply one among many in the various world and international championships.

The West

The beginnings of karate in the West are to be found in Hawaii and California. Large migrations of Chinese workers introduced Chinese systems to the USA in the nineteenth century, but in general these systems were only taught to Chinese in secret, and were not known to the Caucasian population, although sometimes the methods were displayed in exhibitions as part of the Chinese New Year celebrations. In 1922 the Chinese Physical Culture Association was established in Hawaii. This body organized formal ch'uan-fa (Chinese boxing) classes for its members and introduced a variety of methods to Hawaii. Gradually the exclusive nature of the instruction changed and non-Chinese students were admitted; the first instructor to open his classes to the public was Tinn Chan Lee, a Tai-chi-ch'uan instructor, who began to accept non-Chinese students in 1957. Karate had been taught and practised among the Okinawan immigrants to Hawaii, the Okinawans and Japanese forming 40 per cent of the total population of Hawaii in 1900. In 1927 Kensu Yabu taught karate in Hawaii to Okinawans and presented a public demonstration in Honolulu. Yabu's visit resulted in a growth of interest among both Okinawan and non-Okinawan observers and various groups began to form to practise karate. This in turn led to further visits by other Okinawan teachers, perhaps the most famous being the creator of Goju Ryu, Chojun Miyagi, who stayed in Hawaii from May 1934 to January 1935.

The Second World War interrupted any further growth of karate in Hawaii, but after the war a new art emerged, known as Kosho Ryu kempo. Kempo (fist way) is the Japanese reading of the Chinese ch'uan-fa, and was originally taught by James Mitose in the late 1930s and early 1940s. Kempo claims to be a Japanese system based on Chinese Shaolin, but detailed examination of its history and techniques reveals a strong Okinawan influence. It seems more reasonable to see kempo as a fusion of Okinawan karate with Japanese ju-jutsu. Kempo spread rapidly, absorbing techniques and concepts from a variety of other martial arts. It spread to the mainland in the 1950s, mainly through the efforts of Ed Parker, who now heads his own International Kempo Karate Association. The original system introduced by Mitose is now taught by the International Kosho-Shorei Association based in California.

In the 1950s and 1960s, Okinawan, Japanese, Chinese and Korean methods were introduced to the USA through the efforts of returning servicemen who had served in the Orient. This led to the formation of large associations which imported high-ranking Oriental teachers into the USA in order to teach and spread their own methods. All the major styles of Okinawan and Japanese karate are now well represented in the USA, and a large number of highly skilled non-Oriental practitioners are to be found.

In Europe the first karate schools were established in France. Henri Plee, a judo instructor, was instrumental in organizing classes and importing highly ranked Japanese instructors to teach the art. In the 1960s, the art began to spread and soon dojos could be found in most major European countries. In Britain the first dojos were organized in the early 1960s, sometimes based in existing judo and kendo clubs. In Scotland T. Morris began teaching karate, originally going to Paris to study with Henri Plee. In April 1964 a demonstration of Wado Ryu was presented by a team of Japanese instructors led by

Tatsuo Suzuki, then fifth dan. This led to the creation of the All Britain Karate Do Association with Mr Suzuki as the chief instructor. Other associations were established and senior Japanese instructors arrived, most notably Hirokazu Kanazawa, who taught the Shotokan style. Competitions were organized, the first British championships taking place in 1965 at Crystal Palace. Karate grew rapidly and books and magazines were published to supply information and equipment needed by the followers of the art. In the first edition of the magazine *Karate and Oriental Arts* (May 1966) it is stated that there were over fifty clubs in Britain, most of which belonged to the ABKA. The rate of increase was phenomenal and by May 1967 it was possible to hold a European championships in London. Most of the major styles were represented in Britain by the late 1960s with the exception of the Okinawan schools. As Okinawan karate does not put any stress or value on competition karate, there was no way for the Okinawan systems to spread. It is noticeable that British karate was introduced as a competitive sport and is taught with competition as the end result. This resulted in the British team developing into one of the strongest in the world.

The Major Styles of Karate

Shorin Ryu

Okinawan karate can be divided into two main groups – Shorin Ryu, which developed in the towns of Shuri and Tomari (and is therefore sometimes known as Shuri-te) and Naha-te, which developed in the town of Naha. Naha-te includes Goju Ryu and Uechi Ryu, while Shuri-te is represented by a number of groups all known as Shorin Ryu.

The roots of all the Shorin Ryu groups can be traced back to a group of important nineteenth-century teachers, who included Chotoku Kyan (1870–1945), Yasutsune Itosu (1830–1915) and Kentsu Yabu (1863–1937). The senior students of these masters went on to form different groups, which differ only in minor details of the techniques. The main Shorin Ryu groups are:

Kobayashi Ryu (Young Forest Style). Created by Choshin Chibana

(1887–1969) in 1933. Chibana studied under Itosu and, after Gichin Funakoshi took up residence in Japan, was considered to be the senior student in the Itosu line. The leading teacher of this system now is Shugoro Nakazato.

Shobayashi Ryu (Small Forest Style). Created by Chotoku Kyan as an attempt to preserve Itosu's methods unchanged. The leading teacher now is Eizo Shimabuku.

Matsubayashi Ryu (Pine Tree Forest Style). Created by Shoshin Nagamine (born 1907). He studied karate under Taro Shimabuku, Ankichi Arakaki, Chotoku Kyan and Choki Motobu. He chose the name Matsubayashi in memory of two great karate masters, Sokon Matsumura of Shuri (1797–1889) and Kosaku Matsumora of Tomari (1829–98).

Matsumura Shorin Ryu. Created by Hohan Soken, grandson of Sokon Matsumura. This group is now led by Hohan Soken's senior student, Fusei Kise.

The stances of Shorin Ryu are high when compared with Japanese styles. Kicking techniques are aimed at targets below the waist, as Shorin Ryu teachers regard high kicks as dangerous to the attacker as they put the balance at risk and expose the groin to attack. The katas practised by most of the Shorin Ryu groups include: Pinan 1–5, Naihanchi 1–3, Ananku, Rohai, Wankan, Wanshu, Passai (Bassai), Gojushiho, Chinto and Kusanku.

Some groups also practise less well-known kata; for example, Hohan Soken's students practise a semi-secret kata known as the White Crane (Haku Tsuru), taught only to the higher grades.

As well as empty-hand methods, many Shorin Ryu dojos also teach traditional Okinawan weapons. It is quite common to see the *bo, sai, tonfa, kama* and *nunchaku* taught by Shorin Ryu instructors, as they tend to regard those systems which do not train with weapons as incomplete. It is noticeable that the Naha-te schools also train with these weapons, thus showing a possible Shorin Ryu influence. As well as the more common weapons, some instructors teach the use of the oar (*kai* or *eku*), spindle (*techu*), shield and spear (*timbei* and *rochin*) and the knuckleduster (*tekko*). All these weapons have specific kata designed to exploit the specific strengths of each weapon.

Isshin Ryu

Isshin Ryu (One Heart Style) was created by Tatsuo Shimabuku

(1906–75) in 1954. He began to learn karate in 1914, joining his uncle's dojo, where he learned the basics of Shorin Ryu. Later he became a student of Chotoku Kyan, the leading Shorin Ryu teacher in Okinawa, and also studied Goju Ryu from the founder of the style, Chojun Miyagi. According to Steve Armstrong, an eighth dan in Isshin Ryu, Shimabuku also studied kobujutsu (classical weapons) under Shinken Taira and Moden Yabiku, the leading teacher on Okinawa.

Taking what he considered the best from both styles and adding his own interpretations of kata and basic techniques, Shimabuku created his own system in 1954. At first he was not looked on favourably by the followers of the more established methods, but he soon attracted a number of loyal students, including many American soldiers and marines stationed on Okinawa. Some of these men achieved high grades and spread Isshin Ryu to the USA, where it now has many followers.

Shimabuku selected seven kata from Shorin Ryu and Goju Ryu for his style and created one himself. The kata are Seisan, Seiunchin, Naihanchi, Wanshu, Chinto, Sanchin, Kusanku and Sunsu. There are also two prearranged sparring sets which feature *bo* against *bo* and *sai* against *bo*.

Isshin Ryu uses typical Okinawan stances, but concentrates on using the standing fist in punching, and blocking with the muscular areas of the forearm, i.e. the wrist does not twist so as to turn the forearm, but stays in a vertical position. Isshin Ryu practitioners believe that this is a more effective way to block and punch. In general, kicks are kept below the waist, but due to experience gained in competitions some Isshin Ryu stylists in the USA also use kicks to the head.

The style is now headed by Kichiro Shimabuku, the son of the founder. He is assisted by his brother-in-law, Angi Uezu.

Goju Ryu

Goju Ryu (Hard Soft Style) is the name given to the style of karate created by the Okinawan master, Chojun Miyagi (1888–1953). He began to study karate in 1902 under the great Naha-te master Kanryo Higaonna until 1915 when Higaonna died. Miyagi visited China in 1915 and 1917 to study Chinese methods. It seems likely that he studied Fukien White Crane, as that is the system which most closely resembles Goju Ryu. It is often claimed that he studied pa-kua, but there is little or no evidence to prove this assertion; certainly Goju Ryu techniques do not resemble pa-kua to any great extent. Possibly Miyagi studied some of the internal systems in the 1930s when he visited the famous Ching Wu school in Shanghai. While it may have influenced his ideas there is little sign of the internal in Goju Ryu now. Miyagi began teaching karate in 1917 at the Commercial High School in Naha and at the Okinawa Normal College. In 1928 Miyagi visited Japan and taught at various universities. Gogen Yamaguchi, the future leader of Japanese Goju-kai, received some instruction during Miyagi's four-month visit. In 1929 Miyagi decided to name his style Goju Ryu, taking the name from a poem found in an Okinawan martial arts book, the *Bubishi*. The word *goju* means hard/soft, and describes the essential nature of the style which is to harmonize hard and soft movements, i.e. attacking movements are classified as *go* (hard), and tend to be linear, whereas defensive actions are *ju* (soft) and are characterized by curved or circular movements. The kata practised in Goju Ryu are: Gekisai 1 & 2, Saifa, Seiyunchin, Shisochin, Sanseiryu, Seisan, Seipai, Kururunfa, Suparunpei, Sanchin and Tensho.

Some Okinawan instructors also teach Fukyu 1 & 2 as beginners' kata. The style features the extensive use of the Sanchin and Neko Ashi (cat) stances and is generally considered to be a close-in fighting system. The original Okinawan school does not stress competition fighting but the Japanese Goju-kai has adopted many of the practices and attitudes of the other Japanese styles and is involved in competitions to some extent. As well as practising the usual range of karate techniques, followers of Okinawan Goju Ryu also train with a variety of implements designed to improve strength, stamina and impact. These include the *makiwara* (punching post), *chi-ishi* (strength stone), *kame* (jar) and *kongoken* (iron ring). A great deal of attention is directed to developing grip strength, as the style features a wide range of locking and throwing techniques. Free sparring includes attacks to the groin and ground fighting. Of all the major styles, Goju Ryu is one of the least influenced by sporting considerations and for that reason has not widely spread in its pure form in the West. In the USA there are many schools teaching methods loosely based on Goju Ryu, but drastically modified to suit American tournament conditions and the ideas of the various instructors and creators of these new systems.

Uechi Ryu

Uechi Ryu was created by Kanbun Uechi (1877–1945), an Okinawan who studied Chinese boxing at the Central Temple in Fukien Province, China, from 1897–1910. He became the student of a Chinese master, Chou Tze-ho, a famous practitioner of southern-style ch'uan-fa. Chou Tze-ho (1874–1926) was born into a wealthy family in the town of Nanyu. He studied ch'uan-fa under two well-known teachers, Chou Pei from Fukien, a teacher of southern Shaolin boxing, and Ko Hsi T'i from Shantung. Chou Tze-ho's father erected a training hall in his home and invited Ko Hsi T'i to teach his son. The hall is still standing today. In time Chou Tze-ho became well known for the power of his 'iron palm', and for his ability in Tiger boxing, one of the 'Five Fists of Fukien', i.e. Dragon, Tiger, Leopard, Snake and Crane. As well as his martial skills, he was also an accomplished calligrapher, often being asked to write signs or paint for a special purpose. After training for thirteen years, Uechi left China and returned to Okinawa to get married and settle down as a farmer. He did not teach karate, but it is said that many people knew of his ability because a Chinese tea merchant from Fukien, Wu Hsien-kuei (the Japanese pronunciation is Gokenkin), who had met Uechi in China told the Okinawans of Uechi's skills. In 1924, Uechi moved to Wakayama, where he began to teach a young Okinawan named Ryuko Tomoyose. Soon the numbers grew and Uechi opened a dojo. In 1947 he returned to Okinawa where he died the following year. His son, Kanei Uechi, became head of the style which was now known as Uechi Ryu. Prior to this the expression *pangai noon* had been used to describe this art. Taken from the Chinese boxing styles of Fukien, it means 'half hard, half soft' and is used to signify the union of hard and soft techniques common to all Naha-te systems.

There are eight kata taught by the Uechi Ryu; three of them, Sanchin, Seisan and Sanseiryu, were brought to Okinawa by Kanbun Uechi, while the others were created by his son. The kata are as follows: Sanchin, Kanshiwa, Konshu, Seichin, Seisan, Seirui, Konchin, Sanseiryu.

The style is based on Sanchin stance and features a wide range of blocks, strikes and kicks. One interesting point is that Uechi Ryu practitioners can deliver very strong kicks with the tips of the toes! Naturally a great deal of training is required before this can be done without damage to the feet. It is also noticeable that more and more Okinawan/Japanese elements are being added to the style, i.e. use of the *makiwara, chi-ishi* and *kame,* and the use of *mawashi-geri* (roundhouse kick) and competition-derived techniques; in fact, Uechi Ryu fighters are very successful in Okinawan competitions. However, for the purists, competition is merely a step on the way; for them the essence of Uechi Ryu is trying to master Sanchin kata. It is reported that Kanbun Uechi regularly told his students that 'all is Sanchin'; this parallels the attitude of the Goju Ryu teachers and interestingly enough is repeated by teachers of Fukien White Crane ch'uan-fa who say that, of all the kata, Sanchin is the most important.

Uechi Ryu is well established in the USA, where it is under the direction of George Mattson. In Britain, Dave Scott, Ron Ship, Dan Haigh and Harry Benfield are the senior instructors, Dave Scott having spent some time training in Okinawa as a member of Kanei Uechi's dojo. The compilers of this book are both students of Uechi Ryu. Dave Scott (fourth dan) is co-founder of the British Uechi Ryu Association and Mick Pappas (third dan) is its secretary.

Shotokan

One of the most popular styles in the world today, Shotokan was created by Gichin Funakoshi. He studied karate under Itosu and Azato in Okinawa, and in 1922 was asked to demonstrate and teach karate in Japan. In 1936 he opened a dojo, known as the Shotokan or 'Shoto's Hall' (Shoto was Funakoshi's pen name; as well as being a karate master he also wrote poetry in the Chinese style). Initially the style he taught resembled the karate of Okinawa, but over the years a distinctive style evolved. His son Yoshitaka (Giko) Funakoshi was largely responsible for introducing new ideas and techniques, and it is obvious from old photographs that modern Shotokan is based on Yoshitaka Funakoshi's ideas.

The style is characterized by deep stances and powerful expansive movements. All the kata feature long, low movements, performed with a lot of strength, so giving the style a very dynamic appearance. While a great deal of stress is placed on the kata, it is also true to say that many of the movements are performed more for aesthetic purposes than functional ones.

Shotokan in Japan was reorganized after the war. Gichin Funakoshi was too old to do a lot of teaching and the technical development of the style devolved to his senior students, who included Masatoshi Nakayama, Isao Obata and Shigeru Egami. They formed the Japan Karate Association to promote and regulate Shotokan but after Funakoshi's death in 1957 many of the older teachers broke away and formed the Shotokai, claiming that the type of karate being developed by the JKA was not in line with the ethical and moral teachings stressed by Funakoshi; they did not approve of the stress on sparring or of the severity of some of the teaching methods.

The JKA continued under the leadership of Masatoshi Nakayama, developing a group of professional instructors who spread the style around the world. One of the most senior of them, Hirokazu Kanazawa, left the JKA to form his own organization, Shotokan Karate International, which has members throughout the world.

There is no doubt that the efforts of the JKA raised the standards of karate technique. It is said that when Funakoshi first arrived in Japan he only felt able to demonstrate Kusanku (Kanku-dai). He had no real knowledge of the five Pinan (Heian) kata, as he had never learned them from Itosu, because they were created by Itosu for schoolchildren after Funakoshi had ended his formal period of instruction. For this reason he recruited Shinken Gima to assist him on his first demonstration as Gima was proficient at Naihanchi. While these facts may be disturbing to those who regard Funakoshi as a karate genius, they are indicative of the early standard of karate in Japan. It is also said that Funakoshi was surprised at the intensity of judo training at the Kodokan; he had seen nothing like it on Okinawa!

The kata practised by Shotokan karate-ka are: Taikokyu Shodan (also known as Kihon kata), Heian 1–5, Tekki 1–3, Bassai-dai, Bassai-sho, Kanku-dai, Kanku-sho, Gojushiho-dai, Gojushiho-sho, Empi, Hangetsu, Sochin, Jion, Jiin, Jitte, Nijushiho, Chinte, Gangaku, Wankan, Unsu.

Training in Shotokan today is based on a well-regulated procedure. The first stage is to develop strong, precise, well-balanced basic techniques. The five Heian kata are stressed and before a student can be awarded the grade of brown belt he or she must be competent in these five kata and Tekki Shodan. After third kyu (brown belt), training concentrates on developing skill in combination techniques and semi-free sparring, with the emphasis put on Bassai-dai, Empi, Hangetsu, Sochin, Kanku-dai and Jion. After the award of first dan, the student is expected to develop his ability in sparring and in the advanced kata. Initially self-defence methods were also taught, but this is gradually being phased out or relegated to a secondary position in favour of sparring, with the emphasis on scoring points. Shotokan is noted for the importance it places on the development of good form in basic techniques; because of this it has influenced the development of many other systems. It is noticeable, for example, that the kata used by the Goju-kai in competition show a definite Shotokan influence in the whole feeling of the performance; in other words, aesthetic rather than practical considerations are brought to the fore.

Wado Ryu

Wado Ryu, the way of harmony, was created by Hironori Otsuka, one of Gichin Funakoshi's senior students. Otsuka was born in 1892 and began his study of the martial arts as a child. He joined the Shinto Yoshin Ryu school of ju-jutsu at the age of thirteen, where as well as the usual throwing and locking techniques he also studied the system's specialities, striking the *atemi* (vital points) with kicks and punches. In 1921, aged twenty-nine, he became the head of Shinto Yoshin Ryu, taking over from Yukiyoshi Tatsusaburo Nakayama, his own instructor.

When Funakoshi began demonstrating and teaching in 1922, Otsuka became one of the first students. He was aged thirty and a master in his own right, and it did not take him long to assimilate Funakoshi's teachings and methods. Otsuka always showed an interest in kumite (sparring) rather than kata and, although he often assisted Funakoshi in teaching, he was one of the people who developed the modern sparring methods in use today.

In 1934 he set up his own style, naming it the Karate Promotion Club. The style was based on the techniques taught by Gichin Funakoshi, plus some influence from Choki Motobu and Kenwa Mabuni; there is some evidence that Otsuka was influenced by Motobu's ideas on sparring and Mabuni's ways of performing the kata. As well as the Okinawan influence, Otsuka drew upon his knowledge of ju-jutsu to incorporate wristlocks, throws and techniques of avoidance. All in all, he produced the first modern system of karate. In 1940 the Butokukai requested all its members to give the name and founder of the style they practised. Otsuka named his style Wado Ryu, meaning the way of harmony. The name cleverly related to Funakoshi's ethical teachings, and at the same time identifies the school as Japanese, *wa* or harmony being a very important ideal in Japanese society.

The style is built around nine basic kata: Pinan 1–5, Naihanchi, Kushanku, Seishan, Chinto. Some teachers of Wado Ryu include other kata drawn from Okinawan schools, such as Jitte, Niseishi, Rohai and Sanchin.

While the kata are considered valuable, the real heart of the style is best seen in the eight Ohyo Gumite, or prearranged sparring methods. It is here that Otsuka's ideas can be really seen. In a sense these are the true kata of Wado Ryu. Technically Wado Ryu features higher stances than Shotokan, as mobility and avoidance is stressed. There is less obvious use of the hips in punching and blocking, and senior students concentrate on developing a fast whiplash type of punch and kick. These characteristics made it a very successful competition style, leading to it being widely accepted by foreign countries. Wado Ryu has influenced the free-fighting methods used by all competitors, especially in the use of the *mawashi-geri*.

In 1982 Otsuka died. Wado Ryu is now organized into a number of different associations, some of which are changing the style in the light of modern competition needs. The kata are being modified, due to the predominance of Shotokan values, and new kata are being created. There is no doubt that Japanese Wado Ryu and European Wado Ryu are different, probably due to the difference in physique of the practitioners. The style is now headed by the founder's son, Jiro Otsuka, but technically the leading teachers are probably Tatsuo Suzuki and Toru Arakawa.

Shito Ryu

Created by Kenwa Mabuni (1893–1957), Shito Ryu is one of the major styles of karate practised in Japan. Kenwa Mabuni studied karate under Yasutsune Itosu and Kanryo Higaonna, the leading karate masters in Okinawa at the turn of the century; in fact, the name Shito is derived from two of the characters used to write Itosu and Higaonna. Following the lead of Gichin Funakoshi, Mabuni began teaching karate in mainland Japan in 1929, opening his dojo, the Yoshukan, in Osaka in 1934. Mabuni also studied Okinawan weapons, mainly the *sai, bo, tonfa, kama* and *nunchaku*, from Aragaki, a leading Okinawan teacher.

Of all the Japanese and Okinawan styles, Shito Ryu teaches the greatest number of kata, including as it does all the Itosu and Higaonna forms, all the kata taught by the Shorin Ryu, Shotokan and Goju schools. As well as the traditional kata, Mabuni also created some which are unique to Shito Ryu. A book on Shito Ryu kata by Ryusho Sakagami, a leading teacher of the style, includes thirty-eight kata and the list is by no means complete. Some authorities list over fifty kata, not including weapons kata. Basic techniques resemble Shotokan to some extent, except that the stances are not as low and more use is made of Sanchin and Neko Ashi stances.

After Mabuni's death the style split into various independent groups and associations headed by Mabuni's senior students. One of these groups, led by Chojiro Tani, concentrated on developing a style aimed at competition fighting. After a great deal of research and experimentation, a method known as Shukokai was produced, featuring high stances, simplified direct-blocking methods and fast kicking and punching techniques. Due to its success in tournaments, this form of Shito Ryu is the version best known in the West. Shukokai kata, while being based on older Okinawan models, have been changed to conform to the dictates of competition technique.

One of Tani's students, Yoshinao Nanbu, broke away from Shukokai to found his own system known as Sankukai. He did this as he found the stress on competition too limiting and not in keeping with his view of martial arts. Later Nanbu created another system now known as Nanbu-do.

The original Shito Ryu is now beginning to spread to Europe through the efforts of a number of Japanese teachers. In America Shito Ryu is quite well established, the best-known teacher being Fumio Demura.

Kyokushinkai

Created by one of the most interesting and controversial modern martial artists, Mas Oyama, Kyokushinkai is one of the best-known styles in the world. Originally named Choi Young-li, Oyama was born in Korea in 1923. He studied Chinese and Korean systems of combat before moving to Japan where he studied Shotokan under Gichin Funakoshi for a short time and Goju Ryu with a Korean teacher, Neichu So. He was also associated with Gogen Yamaguchi for a while.

Apparently Oyama was not over-impressed with the combat effectiveness of the systems he studied. He retired to the mountains in Chiba prefecture where he trained intensively for a year and a half. Later he toured the USA, where he fought boxers, professional wrestlers and rough-house brawlers. Not content with this, Oyama also fought a number of bulls, killing three with a combination of striking and grappling techniques. He began teaching karate in 1946, eventually creating his own system in 1956. The name selected for this system, Kyokushinkai, means 'the ultimate truth style'; from its inception Oyama intended his system to be as realistic as possible, the stress was on combat effectiveness and fighting, rather than health or character development. Initially Oyama taught a range of kata derived from the Shotokan and Goju schools, including Pinan 1–5, Saifa, Seiyunchin, Sanchin and Tensho. However, in the 1960s and 1970s the role of kata was played down and the techniques and training methods taught at the Kyokushinkai headquarters began to resemble Thai kickboxing more than anything else. Oyama introduced his 'knockdown' concept, allowing heavy contact to the body with a wide range of techniques. With this approach, the fighters are allowed to hit hard, the winner being the last man left standing, although of course some restrictions are imposed: punches cannot be directed to the face, the joints may not be attacked and no attacks to the groin are permitted. However, there is no doubt that fighters trained under this system are effective and have a realistic appreciation of the demands of combat.

Oyama's introduction of this new approach alienated some of his former students, who did not wish to change their style. From their point of view, Kyokushinkai had ceased being karate and had become a type of kickboxing. Some of these people created new associations, while others joined other styles, Okinawan Goju Ryu being one of the most favoured. According to Oyama, Kyokushinkai is the only true martial art left. He denigrates all other Japanese styles, calling them 'karate dancing', and believes that his open championships are the only true tests of fighting ability. In this he has never changed; there are many stories of Oyama challenging rival karate teachers in the 1950s to prove the value of his system and his right to a high grade in karate. He is a direct and forthright man, and while his attitude may cause annoyance in some quarters, there is no doubt that he is sincere in his views. Oyama's approach provides an interesting contrast to the machinations of various 'karate politicians' involved in sport karate.

Training in Kyokushinkai is severe and features a high level of conditioning. The development of a strong fighting spirit is encouraged and is tested frequently. One of the most severe tests is known as the '100-man kumite', which involves fighting 100 times against a wide range of opponents. This feat has been accomplished by a number of Westerners, including the senior Kyokushinkai instructor in Britain, Steve Arneil. Oyama, unlike other oriental teachers, applies a consistent set of rules and values when awarding high grades, a practice which earned him a lot of criticism from various Japanese karate teachers in the 1950s and 1960s. However, his attitude ensures that in general his senior foreign students remain loyal to him as they can see that they are not discriminated against. This probably stems from the fact that he is a Korean and so has experienced the Japanese prejudice against foreigners, which often means that foreign karate-ka are not allowed to progress to the higher grades, irrespective of their skills or knowledge. So, for example, while there are several Westerners with the grades of sixth or seventh dan in Europe who are Kyokushinkai teachers, there are only a small number of other stylists with the same grade. This is because the Japanese parent associations apply different criteria to foreigners than to Japanese when it comes to awarding high grades. The wisdom of Mas Oyama's approach may be observed in the fact that in general Kyokushinkai has seldom suffered from splinter groups breaking away from the parent body, whereas almost all of the other styles periodically suffer from numbers of senior students leaving to create new associations, due to the restrictive policies and attitudes of the controlling Japanese groups.

There are many other styles of karate taught in Okinawa, Japan, and the West, but for reasons of space they cannot all be discussed. However, they all, in one way or another, will be connected with the main systems described here.

The Emergence of Sport Karate

In the 1920s the first generation of Japanese karate-ka began to experiment with sparring methods. Many of them had been exposed to judo and kendo, and so the first efforts to develop sparring methods showed the influence of these martial arts. Interestingly enough, the first type of sparring developed seems to have resembled the modern contact sparring rather than the point sparring now used. There are photographs of Japanese karate-ka taken in the 1920s and 1930s which show them wearing padded armour, boxing gloves and protective helmets. These developments were intended to improve the Okinawan art by introducing a new element to the training; there was no intention to stage public performances.

Sparring in armour never became really popular among the various karate styles, although some groups developed it and continue to the present day. Although many of the older Okinawan teachers were emphatically against sparring, claiming that kata were sufficient for self-defence, the Japanese teachers and students continued to develop sparring methods. Some of the fighting in the thirties and forties was very rough. According to Taiji Kase, broken ribs, smashed teeth and eye damage were not uncommon. To minimize the injuries, various instructors drew up codes of rules, listing acceptable and illegal techniques and defining scoring areas. It also became illegal to strike an opponent intentionally with a powerful technique. So the essence of the art changed and the students were now taught how not to hit hard, instead of the Okinawan ideal of destroying an enemy with one blow.

Once this development had taken place it became possible to stage matches between different styles. This in turn led to the establishment of regular area and national competitions and the emergence of karate champions. By the sixties, success in competition became the standard for judging the skill of an individual and the strength of his style or association. When karate was exported to the West, this process was accelerated, until one of the requirements for a high rank in karate was the ability to be successful in tournaments. Many Japanese karate masters have claimed that they were responsible for developing competition karate, but the truth of the matter is that no single individual was responsible. It was the result of the efforts of a number of people and was almost bound to happen once karate was exposed to the influence of judo and kendo.

In America, competition was the vehicle by which karate spread and even Okinawan styles were modified so that they could take part. However, there was a growing feeling of dissatisfaction with the no-contact rule and in the 1970s a new form of competition emerged, full contact, with the fighters wearing boxing gloves and foot pads. Victory in a karate match no longer depended on the subjective decision of judges and referees, but on the knockout of one of the fighters. Within a short time the proponents of this 'new' method divorced themselves from their karate backgrounds and looked to boxing for punching techniques and training methods, the style resembling boxing with the addition of some kicking techniques. The best of the Americans have fought and defeated Japanese and Thai kickboxers.

The mainstream form of competition karate adheres to the no-contact rule. In the beginning Japanese fighters dominated the championships, but in the Second World Championships (1972), the Japanese team was beaten by the British team, the championship being won by France. Since then the Japanese have never really dominated the fighting section of competition karate, although they reign supreme in kata competition.

Nowadays all the major styles in Japan and the West are actively involved in promoting competition karate, although many Okinawan teachers do not regard competition as a serious endeavour. There are a variety of national and international organizations, all claiming to represent the 'true' voice of karate. The lure of entry into the Olympic Games has forced some degree of cooperation among the various international bodies, but with such a tremendous amount of prestige at stake it is not easy to resolve all the disagreements.

To a traditionalist it is all irrelevant, as karate was never considered to be a sport and any tendency to promote it in such a way must be resisted. To those who see karate as a sport, entry into the Olympics must be the logical thing to aim for. If and when this happens karate will most probably divide into two basic types; the traditional, with equal stress on self-defence and self-improvement, and the modern, with the achievement of winning an Olympic gold medal as its aim. The modern approach is actually leading to the creation of a specific competition style in which the characteristics of the fighter's basic style vanish, to be replaced with a relaxed stance and fluid punches and kicks. As power is no longer a consideration, speed and timing are stressed, and all in-fighting and ground-fighting techniques are ignored. It is important for a beginner to understand what type of dojo he is joining as the techniques which score in a competition are not those which work best in self-defence. For example, under the present World Union of Karate Organizations (WUKO) rules it is illegal to kick an opponent in the groin or attack his joints with strikes or locks; in a real fight these are the techniques which should be used.

Traditional karate will never really become extinct, as many Okinawans and Japanese continue to practise in the time-honoured way. In the West there are those who have retired from competition and see the traditional approach as offering them a new challenge, giving them a reason to continue training. There are also those Westerners who have visited Okinawa and Japan to learn the traditional way. It is through the activities of these individuals that traditional karate will survive alongside the more popular sporting approach.

4 Training Aids and Traditional Equipment

Clothing and practice weapons

One of the nice things about many martial arts is that they can be practised without the need for expensive outfits or equipment. However, some basic requirements are necessary.

The practice of the martial arts is usually a group activity and for this a practice suit, or *gi*, is required. The *gi*, which consists of a jacket, trousers and belt, is similar for most of the martial arts but there are differences which arise from the particular demands of each art. For instance, judo, in which there is a great deal of pulling and tugging, requires a jacket of stronger material than karate, in which there is little grappling. The karate jacket is made of lighter material which gives a characteristic snap when techniques are performed correctly. In aikido, practitioners of shodan (first-degree black belt) and above usually wear *hakama*, a pair of very wide black trousers, with a jacket. Traditionally, kung-fu practitioners have not worn any special or standardized outfits, but some schools are now beginning to use uniforms.

Of the various Eastern martial arts, kendo (Japanese fencing) is really the only one that requires expensive training gear – the headguard, breastplate, gloves, *shinai* (bamboo practice sword), etc. For a beginner, the kendo club will usually have equipment that can be borrowed, but the enthusiast will eventually wish to buy his own gear. He may also, if he practises the kendo kata, wish to buy a wooden training sword (*bokken*) and *katana* (the actual Japanese sword).

Practice weapons will also be required if you wish to practise aikido seriously (the higher grades in aikido practise with the staff and wooden sword) or kobudo, the weapons system associated with karate. For kobudo, the main practice weapons needed are the *sai*, *nunchaku*, *tonfa* and *bo*, which can be obtained from all martial arts supplies shops and companies.

Apart from the clothing and basic equipment, for most of the martial arts special supplementary training equipment is not strictly necessary and, for instance, in tournament karate, judo, aikido and kendo the main form of training is practice with a partner. There is, however, one main exception to this and this is found in the traditional karate of Okinawa and Japan. Since their form of karate stresses the application of direct force to strike and knock down an opponent, various pieces of training equipment have been developed to enhance the power of particular karate techniques. This equipment is discussed below.

Traditional and modern karate training equipment

The makiwara and its variations The *makiwara* is the most important item of training equipment in traditional karate. It is a striking post, about 6 or 7 feet long, of which the lower third is embedded in the ground. The actual striking part of the *makiwara* traditionally consists of a sheaf of straw wrapped tightly with straw rope, but an adequate modern substitute is a pad of rubber. The ideal *makiwara* is neither too stiff nor too springy, but has a certain resilience which pushes back against your strike. The *makiwara* can be used to train any of the basic karate techniques such as the forefist punch, backfist, knifehand and so on. Choki Motobu (1870–1944) even used to train the *ipponken* (one-knuckle fist) on the *makiwara*, but that is very rare.

In the traditional karate of Okinawa and Japan the *makiwara* was considered essential. Today, however, although it is still heavily used in its native Okinawa, only a small proportion of karate students in the West train with it. Many in fact consider it outdated and ineffective. For instance, the *makiwara* is not useful

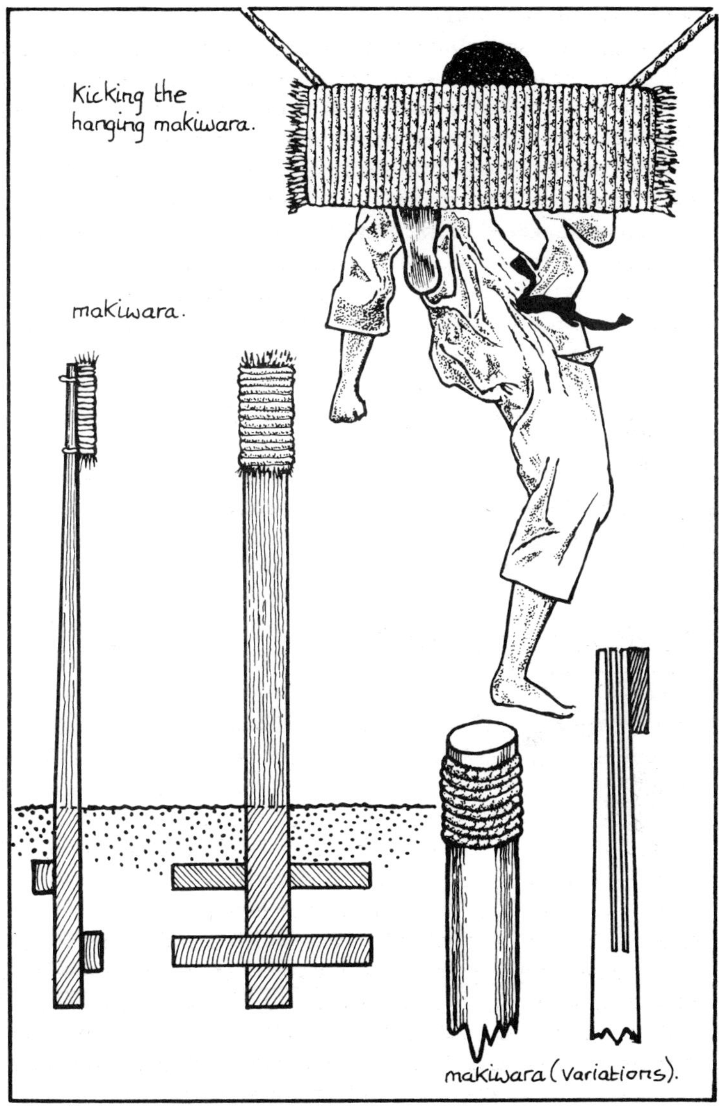
Kicking the
hanging makiwara.
makiwara.
makiwara (variations).

as a training tool for contact karate and is irrelevant to tournament karate where the aim is not destructiveness but catching the opponent with a sharp technique in good form. However, if a student is training in the more traditional form, or for self-defence, then the *makiwara* is a vital training tool. It develops not only power in technique but the strength of the fist, so that it does not buckle on impact, for example, and gives the feeling of actually hitting something, which is very important.

Variations of the *makiwara* include a version with a slot or slots cut in the top of the post (to give a second resistance), and the striking post used to practise blocks and harden the forearms. The hanging *makiwara* (*age-makiwara*) is rarely seen now, having been superseded by the Western punchbag. It consists of a large bundle of straw bound tightly with straw rope. This hanging *makiwara* is used for both striking and kicking. It sometimes has a core filled with sand which brings the weight up to about 60 lb.

The punchbag has been used in karate dojos from about the 1930s, an excellent means of training hands, feet, elbows and knees. Although bag gloves can be worn (as in boxing), many students choose to train on the bag with the naked fist. This is actually more realistic, although it may be more harmful to the hands. One occasionally hears of a hard stylist in kung-fu who fills a punchbag with ball bearings, but this seems to be taking things a little too far.

Spearhand conditioning The fist, backfist, knifehand, etc., are trained on the *makiwara*, but for the spearhand (*nukite*) the traditional training method is to thrust your fingers into a box of sand. Gradually the sand is replaced by beans, and then gravel. Another training tool for *nukite* is a bundle of thin bamboo rods, smoothed and cleaned, and bound together as shown in Figure (p. 91). The *nukite* is thrust into this bundle. The spearhand is used little in modern karate and these methods are now regarded as somewhat antiquated.

Kake-tebiki Another traditional piece of training equipment is the *kake-tebiki*, an instrument used for developing blocking techniques. The wooden 'arm' is blocked and then grasped and pulled down (as Figure (p. 89) shows, a stone provides a counter-

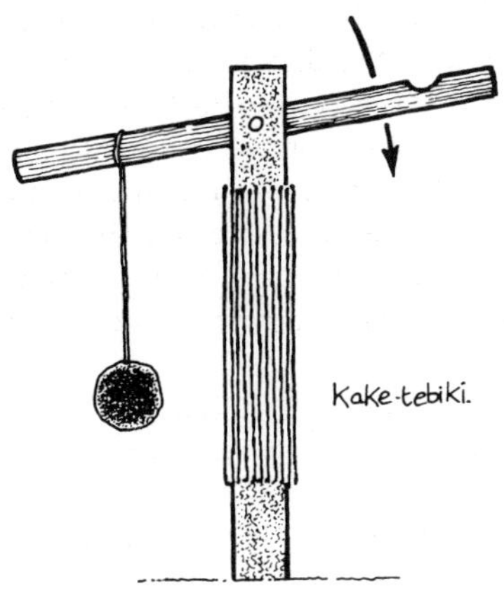

weight), before delivering a counterstrike to the main body which is covered with a bundle of bamboo rods.

Wooden man Some southern styles of kung-fu have an analogous piece of training equipment to the *kake-tebiki*, the so-called 'wooden man', and they have taken its development much further, having developed specific forms for training on the equipment. The best-known example is in the Wing Chun style, where practice on the wooden dummy includes over a hundred techniques, including blocking, grabbing, striking and kicking movements. This serves the purpose of not only hardening the forearms to defend against strong attacks, but also blending together defensive and counter-attacking techniques according to the style's principles. The Choy-Li-Fut kung-fu-style wooden dummy is roughly similar but includes a movable arm similar to the karate *kake-tebiki*.

Traditional weight-training equipment Systematized weight training as such does not form a part of traditional karate. However, certain rather primitive items of equipment are used in some styles to develop the strength of the hands and arms. These items are often constructed from natural materials and a basic form of heavy 'strength stone' is illustrated (Figure (p. 91)). However, the most widely used items of equipment are the

Training with the Tan.
1.
2.
1
3.
Training with the
Kongoken (iron ring).

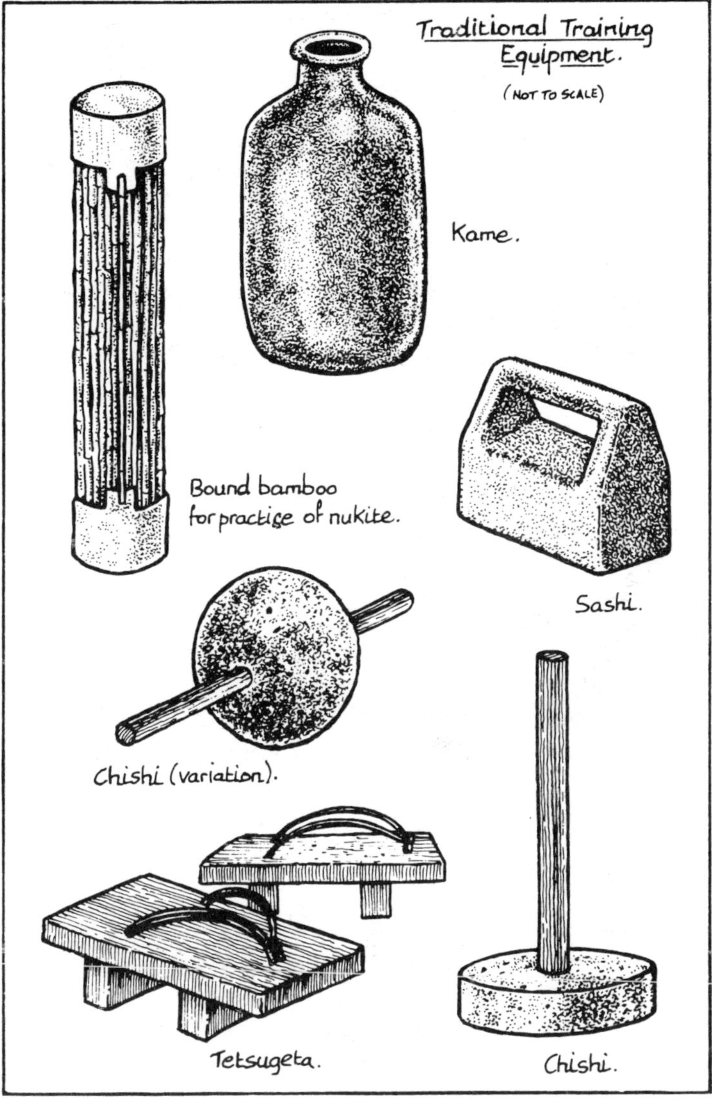
Traditional Training Equipment.
(NOT TO SCALE)
Kame.
Bound bamboo for practice of nukite.
Sashi.
Chishi (variation).
Tetsugeta.
Chishi.

chishi, sashi, kame and *tetsugeka*.

The *chishi* consists of a stone weight (for example) attached to a wooden shaft. An old rule of thumb is that the length of the shaft should be equal to the length of the shinbone. The *chishi* works on the principle of leverage and is manipulated in various ways to develop the strength of the wrist and forearm.

The *sashi* are stone (or iron) weights, usually used in conjunction with karate techniques of thrusting and blocking. They are analogous to modern light dumbells. The *sashi* can also be used for stamping-kick practice (the feet are hooked through the *sashi*), but this is rather clumsy and uncomfortable and for this purpose the *tetsugeka* (iron shoes) are more suitable.

The *kame* is a jar, or more usually two jars, used to develop grip and finger strength. The jars are filled to a suitable weight, then picked up by the karate-ka and carried, usually in a karate stance. As the karate-ka's grip-strength increases, more weight is added to the jars.

To increase the strength of kicks the *tetsugeka* (iron shoes) are used. These are not usually available in the West, but an alternative is the iron boots which are sold with sets of weight-training equipment. Actually, these boots are more comfortable than the *geka*, and more convenient to use.

Tan and kongoken As mentioned previously, weight training as such is not an integral part of karate. However, some Okinawan styles make limited use of the *tan*, a type of barbell weighing 50–60 lb. This weight is too light to use for orthodox weight-training exercises such as the squat, bench press and so on, but the Okinawans use the *tan* in other ways, such as rolling it down the outstretched arms (to toughen up the forearms) or twisting it from side to side. The exercises are usually performed in karate stances and so the practitioner is also able to get some stance training.

One unique piece of training equipment found in the Goju style is the *kongoken* (iron ring). Weighing perhaps 70–80 lb, the *kongoken* is pulled and twisted in various ways (there are two-man exercises also) to develop overall body power.

Modern Japanese training equipment The orthodox form of karate sparring, with no (or slight) contact, does not require any

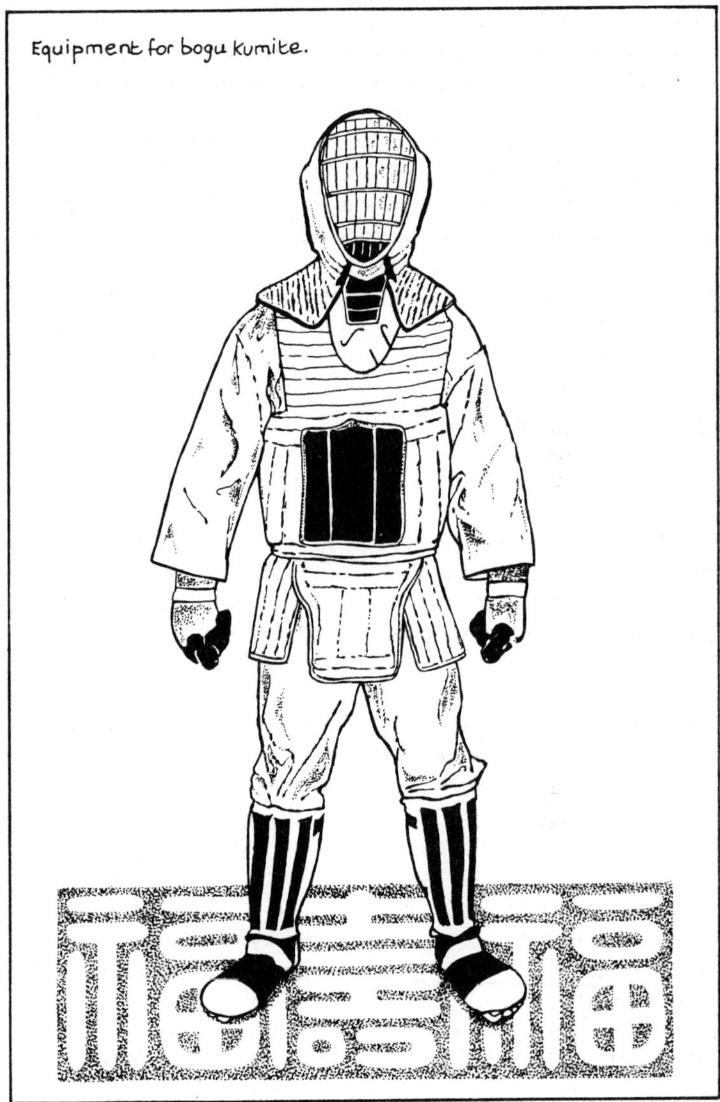

Equipment for bogu kumite.

specific equipment, although wearing shin and groin guards and light hand and foot pads is often advisable. However, in Japan a form of contact sparring has been in existence since *c.* 1930. This is bogu kumite, a type of sparring carried out by contestants wearing full protective gear: a helmet similar to the kendo headguard, body protector, gloves, shin and foot guards. This Japanese equipment is well made and it is very interesting to use for sparring occasionally. However, as well as being expensive, it is relatively cumbersome; the helmet, for example, feels heavy and restrictive. New lines of equipment have recently been brought out in Japan which include lighter and more suitable headguards with a Perspex-type visor.

Modern Western training equipment The modern American form of full-contact karate does not use any protective gear except for boxing gloves and pads to cover the feet. Because of the nature of this contact karate (really a modern combat sport based on a similar principle to Western boxing), its training methods follow, not the methods of traditional karate, but those of boxing. The punchbag, a much more versatile piece of striking equipment, has replaced the *makiwara*, and punchpads ('hook and jab pads') are excellent for developing fluency in punching attacks. To develop kicking techniques the karate-ka can use the punchbag, kicking pads which are held by a partner, and the airbag which contains a cushion of air and was first popularized by Bruce Lee. The airbag is especially useful for side kicks and knee attacks. The main purpose of such equipment is to develop endurance and power in attacking techniques. Skill in contact karate technique comes from sparring practice and for this gloves (including the big 16-oz sparring gloves), footpads and headguard are necessary. Of course, practice in a boxing ring is essential for anyone wanting to take up the sport seriously.

Conclusion Special training equipment is not necessary for many of the martial arts, and if you are practising simply for flexibility and fitness the movements of these arts are sufficient in themselves. If you are practising a sport such as judo or tournament karate, then the main requirement is sufficient training and sparring partners. For traditional karate and self-defence some degree of power development and body conditioning is necessary, and the *makiwara*, *chishi*, etc., are very useful training implements. For contact karate, conditioning is a vital factor and the students will need facilities similar to those in a boxing gym.

5 The History of Zen and the Martial Arts

Enlightenment means seeing through to your own essential nature and this at the same time means seeing through to the essential nature of the cosmos and of all things. For seeing through to essential nature is the window of enlightenment. One may call essential nature truth if one wants to. In Buddhism from ancient times it has been called suchness or Buddha-nature or one Mind. In Zen it has been called nothingness, the one hand, or one's original face. The designations may be different, but the content is completely the same.

Quote from Zen master Yasutani

Zen is a practical method of realizing this Buddha-nature, which is the same as one's own essential nature. Zen has no other aim than this. Zen schools have developed training systems based on the practice of za-zen (sitting meditations) or koan study (a koan is a paradox not solvable by rational thought) or both, which over the centuries have proved most successful in helping men and women see through the illusion of their own egos and experience the awe-inspiring realization of their own nature. The training is very hard; it requires much physical and mental discipline; it is anti-intellectual and close to nature; and it is not concerned with material things. Long Zen practice leads to inner strength, freedom from fear and intuitive spontaneity. These were qualities much admired by the samurai of ancient Japan and they became followers of Zen. Later, when the warrior class became the ruling class, Zen became the official state religion (although many would argue that Zen is not a

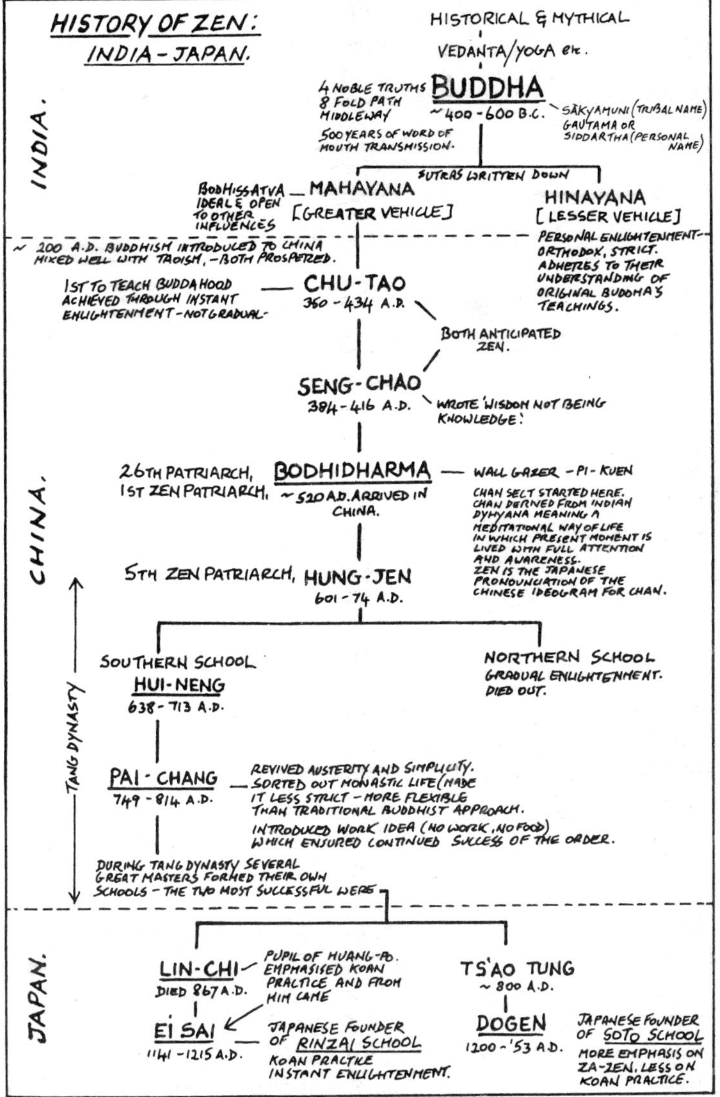
HISTORY OF ZEN:
INDIA - JAPAN.
HISTORICAL & MYTHICAL
VEDANTA/YOGA etc.
INDIA.
4 NOBLE TRUTHS
8 FOLD PATH
MIDDLEWAY
BUDDHA
~400 - 600 B.C.
SĀKYAMUNI (TRIBAL NAME)
GAUTAMA OR
SIDDARTHA (PERSONAL NAME)
500 YEARS OF WORD OF MOUTH TRANSMISSION.
SUTRAS WRITTEN DOWN
BODHISSATVA IDEAL & OPEN TO OTHER INFLUENCES
MAHAYANA
[GREATER VEHICLE]
HINAYANA
[LESSER VEHICLE]
PERSONAL ENLIGHTENMENT - ORTHODOX, STRICT. ADHERES TO THEIR UNDERSTANDING OF ORIGINAL BUDDHA'S TEACHINGS.
~200 A.D. BUDDHISM INTRODUCED TO CHINA MIXED WELL WITH TAOISM, - BOTH PROSPERED.
CHINA.
1ST TO TEACH BUDDAHOOD ACHIEVED THROUGH INSTANT ENLIGHTENMENT - NOT GRADUAL -
CHU-TAO
360 - 434 A.D.
BOTH ANTICIPATED ZEN.
SENG-CHAO
384 - 416 A.D.
WROTE 'WISDOM NOT BEING KNOWLEDGE.'
26TH PATRIARCH,
1ST ZEN PATRIARCH,
BODHIDHARMA
~520 A.D. ARRIVED IN CHINA.
WALL GAZER - PI - KUEN
CHAN SECT STARTED HERE. CHAN DERIVED FROM INDIAN DYHYANA MEANING A MEDITATIONAL WAY OF LIFE IN WHICH PRESENT MOMENT IS LIVED WITH FULL ATTENTION AND AWARENESS. ZEN IS THE JAPANESE PRONOUNCIATION OF THE CHINESE IDEOGRAM FOR CHAN.
5TH ZEN PATRIARCH,
HUNG-JEN
601 - 74 A.D.
SOUTHERN SCHOOL
HUI-NENG
638 - 713 A.D.
NORTHERN SCHOOL
GRADUAL ENLIGHTENMENT. DIED OUT.
TANG DYNASTY
PAI-CHANG
749 - 814 A.D.
REVIVED AUSTERITY AND SIMPLICITY. SORTED OUT MONASTIC LIFE (MADE IT LESS STRICT - MORE FLEXIBLE THAN TRADITIONAL BUDDHIST APPROACH.
INTRODUCED WORK IDEA (NO WORK, NO FOOD) WHICH ENSURED CONTINUED SUCCESS OF THE ORDER.
DURING TANG DYNASTY SEVERAL GREAT MASTERS FORMED THEIR OWN SCHOOLS - THE TWO MOST SUCCESSFUL WERE
JAPAN.
LIN-CHI
DIED 867 A.D.
PUPIL OF HUANG-PO. EMPHASISED KOAN PRACTICE AND FROM HIM CAME
EI SAI
1141 - 1215 A.D.
JAPANESE FOUNDER OF RINZAI SCHOOL
KOAN PRACTICE
INSTANT ENLIGHTENMENT.
TS'AO TUNG
~800 A.D.
DOGEN
1200 - '53 A.D.
JAPANESE FOUNDER OF SOTO SCHOOL
MORE EMPHASIS ON ZA-ZEN, LESS ON KOAN PRACTICE.

religion) of Japan. Zen thought influenced all aspects of Japanese life and art and particularly the martial arts.

Samurai warriors used Zen training to condition themselves physically and mentally for battle. The state of consciousness strived for in Zen which results from the stripping away of all conscious ego is both that state which precedes a flash of enlightenment and the one which prepares the warrior perfectly for battle. This seeming paradox of using Zen, which stresses compassion for all sentient beings, for training to kill other human beings is one of the apparent paradoxes that arise in any discussion on Zen. In this case the solution can probably be found in an examination of the practical advantages of Zen training and the different cultural attitudes of then and now. In Zen terms, however, the martial arts should, ideally, be used only as a vehicle to help the practitioner in his or her goal of discovering his or her own true nature. To use Zen methods solely for advancing one's technical expertise in the martial arts or any other field shows a misunderstanding of Zen and will probably lead to failure.

The only way to understand Zen is to practise it in real life and part of this practice may very usefully be the study of one of the martial arts. Reading this chapter cannot substitute for practice but it may prepare the way for practice to start and provide the motivation for the newcomer for further investigation of Zen.

This chapter discusses the origins in Buddhism of Zen, how Zen ideas developed in China, how Zen reached Japan, the two main schools of Zen that resulted, koan and za-zen practice and Zen in the martial arts. At the end of the book are contact addresses for Zen organizations in the West, and a further reading list.

Buddhism, yoga and Zen

The story of Zen starts in India at the time of the Buddha's birth. His teachings, much modified by Zen masters but still the basis of Zen, resulted in part from his reaction to the contemporary teachings of his day. The historical Buddha was born in approximately 560 BC in India. Indian philosophical thought at that time was largely influenced by the Vedas and the science of yoga, although within these two schools there were many different philosophical systems and religious movements. The Buddha followed a number of different teachings but did not find what he was looking for. After much searching he gave up following other teachings and was finally enlightened by his own efforts. His enlightenment resulted in a break with the conventional teachings of his times. He opposed all bodily castigations (much practised by yogis of the time), anything to do with magic (rites, potions, spirtualism, etc.), and, most importantly, he much simplified meditation techniques. Here were the roots of Zen practice.

The other important difference, already evident in the Buddha's teachings, between later Zen thought and traditional Indian yoga is their contrasting interpretations of the enlightenment experience. In classical yoga the self is considered to be spiritually pure and free but in the course of being born becomes caught up or bound to the material world (nature). Each individual's task is to liberate the self from this tie. One way to do this is through the practice of yoga. Thus, in the yogic view enlightenment leads to a totally free autonomous individual self separate from the world. The Buddhist view, as understood by Zen Buddhists, is that there is no division between the self and the world. The universe and everything in it is a seamless whole and to experience enlightenment is to experience this cosmic totality. The self, without the ego getting in the way, can be experienced in its true and numinous nature as in essential relation to all reality.

It is interesting the way these two views are exemplified in Zen and classical yoga meditation techniques. In Zen the meditator keeps his or her eyes half open, that is, he remains part of the world while practising interior calm. In yoga the meditator closes his or her eyes and focuses all attention on inner contemplation, that is, he excludes the world.

Buddhism and Zen

In Zen the historical Buddha, also called Sakyamuni (his tribal name) or Gautama or Siddartha (personal name), should not be confused with mythical Buddhas and other enlightened beings also called Buddha. The Buddha postulated that the way to achieve human happiness and the elevation of suffering was to accept the Four Noble Truths and to follow the Noble Eightfold path and the Middle Way. The Four Noble Truths were: (1) Life is mainly suffering; (2) Suffering is caused by desire for the wrong things; (3) The way to stop suffering is to stop desire; (4) The way to stop desire is to follow the Eightfold Noble Path. These Four Noble Truths, or at least their interpretation (since the Buddha's teachings were not written down until about five hundred years after his death), were later disputed by some Buddhists and are not necessarily accepted by all Zen masters. This is not as out of keeping with the Buddha's teachings as it may at first appear. The Buddha had no intention of creating a rigid system of beliefs and certainly not a religious system. That no truths need to be slavishly adhered to is contained in the following advice given by the Buddha and recorded in the Paranibbana Sutra:

> Be for yourselves your own flame and support. Let the truth be your flame and support, do not seek any other support. He who, from this moment, or after I have disappeared, is his own flame and his own support will be a real disciple of mine, a disciple who knows how to conduct himself well.

Of course, many of the Buddha's successors emphasized particular aspects of his teachings but the importance this gave them reflected personal beliefs rather than universal truths.

The Eightfold Noble Path has generally been accepted in Zen teachings as providing an excellent structure in which to lead a life in tune with Zen ideals. It recommends rightness in: (1) understanding, (2) speech, (3) aspiration, (4) behaviour, (5) livelihood, (6) effort, (7) attentiveness and (8) concentration. Of course, the definition of rightness leaves the meaning of the Eightfold Noble Path open to much debate.

The Middle Way is the path that treads a balance in life, and moderation is the quality to cultivate. Moderation in moderation is also important, hence the occasional instance of Zen masters getting blind drunk!

In practical terms the Zen master will be uninterested in personal views of Buddhist beliefs. With faith in the students' own possible enlightenment and the motivation to practise za-zen with conviction and determination, he knows that they will come naturally to follow the Eightfold Noble Path and the Middle Way.

The First Patriarch

The Buddha was the First Patriarch and his successor, a monk called Mahakasyapa, the Second Patriarch. The story of the succession of Mahakasyapa is traditionally the earliest record of a Zen expression of Truth. The story is related by D. T. Suzuki in the first series of his book *Essays in Zen Buddhism* (Rider, 1950).

> The Buddha was one day on the Mount of Vultures, preaching to a congregation of disciples. He did not resort to a long verbal harangue to explain the subject he was treating. He simply raised up before the assembly a bouquet of flowers that one of his disciples had offered to him. Not a word left his mouth. No one understood the meaning of this attitude except the venerable Mahakasyapa who smiled serenely at the Master, as if he fully understood the meaning of this silent teaching.
>
> The Buddha, noticing this, solemnly proclaimed: 'I have the most precious spiritual treasure which at this moment I am transmitting to you, O venerable Mahakasyapa.'

Mahakasyapa had obviously realized that a flower expressed reality in ways that words could not. The story may or may not be true, but it probably became popular in Zen folklore because it clearly illustrates the later anti-intellectual approach of Zen masters.

Mahayana and Hinayana Buddhism

After his enlightenment the Buddha spent the rest of his life (forty-nine years) as a monk, walking from place to place, preaching his philosophy. The Buddha's teachings continued to spread throughout India after his death but nothing was ever written down and for the next four to five hundred years transmission of Buddhist ideas was by word of mouth. Once the teachings were written down in the form of sutras (a sutra is a text which Buddhists believe reflects the direct teachings of the Buddha himself, although in Indian religion generally a sutra is the writing of any great master), unacknowledged divisions in

Buddhist schools of thought became more obvious. A major split started about four centuries after the Buddha's death and out of it came two major schools of Buddhist thought. The Hinayana or Small Vehicle school and the Mahayana or Great Vehicle school. The former attached much importance to Buddhist texts, orthodox views, rituals and the belief that enlightenment was only possible after extinguishing all worldly needs. The Mahayana school was more open to other influences; it placed little emphasis on texts and rituals and encouraged participation in the world, while at the same time practising non-attachment. It thought desires should be mastered, rather than extinguished, and suffering should be endured, experienced and learned from rather than escaped from. Mahayana Buddhism was the school of thought that spread to China and influenced or catalysed the formation of the school of Ch'an which later became Zen in Japan. In about AD 520 the Buddhist monk Bodhidharma arrived in China from India. He was the Twenty-Sixth Buddhist Patriarch and the First Zen Patriarch. The arrival of Bodhidharma marked the true start of the history of Zen.

Bodhidharma, First Zen Patriarch

Bodhidharma, an Indian Buddhist, arrived in China and travelled to Nanking where he is said to have met the Chinese Emperor Wu-ti. Emperor Wu was a devout Buddhist who had built many temples and in accordance with the teachings of his time assumed he had gained much merit. He was happy to meet this well-known monk and wanted him to know of his spiritual achievements. They are said to have had the following conversation:

Emperor: 'I have built many temples, copied innumerable sacred sutras and initiated many monks since becoming Emperor. Therefore I ask you what is my merit?'

Bodhidharma replied, 'None whatsoever.'

The Emperor persisted and said, 'Why no merit?'

The monk replied, 'Doing things for merit has an impure motive and it will bear only the puny fruit of rebirth.'

The Emperor, a little put out, then asked, 'What then is the most important principle of Buddhism?'

The monk replied, 'Vast emptiness, nothing sacred.'

The Emperor, by now bewildered, then asked, 'Who is it that now stands before me?'

Bodhidharma replied, 'I don't know.'

Realizing that the Emperor was not yet ready for his teaching, the monk left the palace and travelled to the mountains where he became known as Pi-Kuen, the wall-gazer. He is said to have practised intense meditation for nine continuous years. His wisdom and dedication attracted many followers and through his influence the Ch'an sect developed. Ch'an is a Chinese word deriving from the Indian word *dhyana*, meaning a meditational way of life in which the present moment is lived with full attention and awareness. Zen is the Japanese pronunciation of the Chinese ideogram for Ch'an.

The Ch'an Sect

The Ch'an school was anti-intellectual and against any systemization of its teachings. The early Ch'an masters of the T'ang dynasty (AD 618–907) wrote nothing down except for a few brief, cryptic sayings later collected as *Sayings of the Ancient Worthies*.Their teaching methods were influenced by Chinese Taoist thought which believed that the logical constructions of the rational mind are a great block to enlightenment. They began using paradoxes, methods such as talking in nonsensical conundrums, giving beatings at appropriate moments with a stick, or pulling noses or making rude noises to undermine their followers' confidence in rational thought and to induce a state of consciousness ripe for enlightenment. These colourful methods had the wonderful name 'Strange Words and Strange Actions'. Out of them came the later Zen practices of koan study and the mondo sessions in which master and novice have regular question and answer sessions in which the novice's answers in my experience are always wrong. Well, not quite always!

The Ch'an school set its sights on practical realization and against the accumulation of knowledge. It believed that too much emphasis on study of the sutras, too much philosophical discussion and too much sacredness result in a forgetting of the original aim of the whole exercise – enlightenment. To make his point, a master of the T'ang dynasty burned a wooden statue of the Buddha to keep warm on a cold day. Another suggested that if you meet the Buddha on the road and he gets in your way, kill him. The point being that preoccupation with a historical person or a fixed set of ideas can prevent the realization of your own personal and universal self. It is within this context that the Buddhist and Christian views of 'God' become more clearly understood. The Zen view is that the state of Reality is the state of ordinary life and that while one is discussing the concept of God one is missing the experience of (its) Reality. This is perfectly illustrated, in one of my favourite Zen stories, by the experience of a Jesuit monk in a Zen monastery. Here is the story adapted from the version recorded in the book *Zen, Direct Pointing at Reality* by Anne Bancroft (Thames & Hudson, 1979).

Father William Johnston was practising za-zen when the master came along to help him with his posture. The master asked Father Johnston what method of meditation he was using. Father Johnston said he was sitting silently in the presence of God. The master said very good, if you continue doing that God will disappear and only Father Johnston will remain. The Father was a little shocked and said God will not disappear but Father Johnston may well disappear and only God will remain. Yes, yes, replied the master, smiling. That's that I mean, it's the same thing.

Zen and the work principle

Zen continued to thrive in China after the death of the First Patriarch but Zen monks still followed the Indian way of wandering from place to place and begging for their needs. This started to change with the Fourth Patriarch, Tao-hsin, who settled down in one place in a mountainous area of North China and by the time of his death was surrounded by many followers. By the time of the Fifth Patriarch, Hung-jen (AD 601–74), up to a thousand monks were studying Zen in this same area. It became obvious that in the difficult climatic conditions of this not very fertile part of the country the monks had to become self-sufficient in both food and fuel. Hung-jen's followers built a monastery and started to cultivate the land. This was the start of the important Zen tradition that in the search for enlightenment both practical and spiritual activities have to be combined. The idea was more clearly formulated by the master, Pai-chang (AD 749–814), who introduced the famous Zen expression, 'If one does not do any work for a day, one should not eat for a day.' He developed a set of guidelines for monastic life which emphasized austerity and simplicity but at the same time avoided inflexibility and too much attention to rules and regulations. Towards the end of his life Pai-chang still worked in the fields every day. Tradition has it that his followers, fearing for his health, hid his tools so that he could not work. Pai-chang refused to eat until the tools were returned and then he did his stint in the fields.

The Sixth Zen Patriarch

One of the students of the monastery built by Hung-jen was an illiterate peasant boy who was later to become the Sixth Zen Patriarch. His name was Hui-neng and next to Bodhidharma he is perhaps the most revered master in Zen history. In the biographical account of his life and beliefs, the Sutra of Hui-neng, he tells of joining the followers of Hung-jen after overhearing a recital of a passage from the Diamond Sutra. The words 'Depending upon nothing you must find your own mind' filled him with illumination. He joined the monastery but the master, recognizing his brilliance, set him to work in the kitchen to avoid embarrassing the older monks. But eight months later the master called a meeting of all the monks and announced that any monk who could compose a poem that explained the great principle or essence of Buddhism would receive the robe of office and be ordained Sixth Zen Patriarch.

The favourite for the title was the head monk, a man called Shen-hsui. After four days of effort he produced the following verse which he wrote, unsigned, on a corridor wall in the dead of the night:

> Our body is the Bodhi-tree
> And our mind mirror bright.
> Carefully we wipe them hour by hour
> And let no dust alight.

Hui-neng, on passing along the corridor, had the verse read out to him. He dictated a poem to go alongside it:

> There is no Bodhi-tree,
> Nor stand of a mirror bright.
> Since all is void
> Where can the dust alight?

All were amazed and the master, recognizing that this was the work of somebody who truly understood the essence of the Mind, rubbed it out lest it put Hui-neng in danger from jealous monks. Hui-neng was summoned to see the Fifth Zen Patriarch that same night. He was given the robe and begging bowl of office (said to be those of Bodhidharma) and an explanation of the Diamond Sutra. He was then advised to leave the monastery and flee to the south. There followed fifteen years of conscious anonymity and then Hui-neng decided the time was right to reveal himself as the Sixth Zen Patriarch. He became a famous master of Zen and began the southern school of Ch'an which was later transmitted to Japan. The northern school died out and much of contemporary Zen thought is primarily influenced by Hui-neng's teachings and anti-intellectual approach.

Zen reaches Japan

During the time of the T'ang dynasty (AD 618–907) several great masters formed their own schools of Ch'an. Two of the most successful were Lin-chi (born 867) and Ts'ao-tung (born 800). These schools of thought were later transmitted to Japan by two Japanese monks, Eisai (1141–1215), founder of the Rinzai school, and Dogen (1200–1253), founder of the Soto school. Rinzai (Japanese for Lin-chi) and Soto (Japanese for Ts'ao-tung) are the most popular schools of Zen in contemporary Japan. Rinzai Zen emphasizes koan practice and Soto Zen emphasizes sitting meditation (za-zen), although both schools use both techniques.

Eisai in 1194 built the first Zen temple in Japan in Katata. It is called Shofukuji and is still standing. He later moved to Kyoto where he began to create the real foundations of the Rinzai school.

Rinzai Zen

The Rinzai school places emphasis on sudden enlightenment (as opposed to gradual in the Soto school) brought about by long practice of a koan exercise. This sudden flash of awareness is brought about by intense concentration on the koan over a long period of time under stress. Thus the word 'sudden' does not mean that enlightenment is possible without hard work or preparation; rather, there are no degrees of enlightenment, either you are or you are not. The mature student is just as far away as the novice in his experience of enlightenment. He does, however, have more potential for achieving it. One might say that potential accumulates with practice. The koan forces extreme concentration on one thought or question that has no logical answer. It compels a stopping of the rational thought processes and stills the mind of all its conditioned responses, thus allowing an experience of the Reality that underlies all existence.

There are many koans; perhaps the most famous are 'What is the sound of one hand clapping?' and 'Show me your face before your mother and father met', although the koan most often used in Zen practice is the Mu koan.

A monk asked the master Joshu, 'Does a dog have Buddha-nature or not?'

Joshu replied, 'Mu!'

Mu is a word that has no meaning in Japanese. The problem is what is the meaning of Mu.

As I have said earlier, the answer is obviously not a logically correct one but the answer must illustrate that the true essence of Mind or Buddha has been experienced by the student. Thus the answer may not even be verbal.

Two contemporary Zen masters had the following to say about the Mu koan.

Yastutani-Roshi:

> You must concentrate day and night, questioning yourself about Mu through every one of your 360 bones and 84,000 pores. . . . What this refers to is your entire being. Let all of you become one mass of doubt and questioning. Concentrate on and penetrate fully into Mu. To penetrate into Mu is to achieve this unity by holding to Mu tenaciously day and night! Do not separate yourself from it under any circumstances! Focus your mind on it constantly. Do not construe Mu as

nothingness and do not conceive it in terms of existence or non-existence. You must not, in other words, think of Mu as a problem involving the existence or non-existence of Buddha-nature. Then what do you do? You stop speculating and concentrate wholly on Mu – just Mu!

Katsuki Sekida from his excellent book *Zen Training* (Weatherhill, New York, 1975):

Now, 'Mu' means 'nothing' and is the first koan in Zen. You might suppose that, as you sit saying 'Mu', you are investigating the meaning of nothingness. But that is quite incorrect. It is true that your teacher, who has instructed you to work on Mu, may repeatedly say to you, 'What is Mu?' 'Show me Mu,' and so on, but he is not asking you to indulge in conceptual speculation. He wants you to experience Mu. And in order to do this, technically speaking, you have to take Mu simply as the sound of your own breath and entertain no other idea. Only intensely keep on saying 'Mu,' and when you are successful in this practice, quite without any philosophical speculation, you will one day come to realize that the answer is already given, and you will clap your hands and burst out into a great shout of laughter. If, on the other hand, you start trying to think of the meaning of Mu you will lose touch with immediacy and be left all at sea, drifting about bewildered among conceptual ideas.

My own favourite koan and the answer to it by the English Zen commentator R. H. Blyth follow:

Kyogen said, 'It's like a man (a monk) up a tree, hanging from a branch with his mouth; his hands can't grasp a bough, his feet won't reach one. Under the tree there is another man, who asks him the meaning of Daruma's coming from the West. If he doesn't answer he evades his duty. If he answers, he will lose his life. What should he do?'

This problem is a central one in human life, particularly between teacher and pupil, husband and wife, and so on. If we teach, they don't understand. If we don't teach they are dissatisfied. Love is mutual obedience. Also it means teaching the other to love more. If I am always obedient, the other becomes impudent or at least makes no progress. If I demand obedience, love being mutual, the other's love simply decreases. Kierkegaard says that we must believe in the love in the other's heart and thus arouse it. Perhaps this is the answer to Kyogen's problem, but we must not expect any results. Simply believe, that if we open our mouths we won't fall, believe that if we don't open our mouths the other will somehow understand the meaning of the coming of Daruma from the West.

R. H. Blyth was at one time tutor to the Japanese Emperor's son; he had a wonderful but idiosyncratic understanding of Zen. (See his five volumes entitled 'Zen and the Zen Classics',

Hokuseido Press, Tokyo, 1962.)

The Rinzai school was very attractive to the warrior class in the Japan of the twelfth century. They liked the fact that much learning and scholarship might be a block rather than an advantage in the study of Zen. Flashes of enlightenment, quickness of intuition, intense concentration, all these they responded to; no longer did they need to feel inferior to the literary aristocracy. The qualities needed for the battlefield were the same as those needed for the study of Zen. Rinzai flourished with the samurai and Eisai was invited to open a temple in Kamakura, the chosen site for the new warrior capital. Descendants of the warrior class were to rule Japan for the next six centuries and Zen became the 'religion' of the ruling class. Hence the much greater influence of Zen on Japanese culture than that of Ch'an on Chinese culture.

Soto Zen

Dogen, founder of the Soto sect, was born in 1200. His father was an aristocrat but he died when Dogen was two and Dogen's mother died five years later. Dogen was looked after by relatives and at the age of thirteen he went to live with an uncle, a devout Buddhist, who practised a meditative way of life. This experience confirmed in Dogen his decision to become a monk. Some years later he joined the monastery of Kenninjo founded by Eisai and studied with Eisai's successor, Master Myozen. During his time at the monastery Dogen received his *inka*, or the seal of a master, but according to his writings he had still not resolved in himself a basic dilemma. Dogen was bothered by the apparent contradiction that if all human beings are born with Buddha-nature why is it so hard for them to experience authentically this reality?

Dogen's doubts lead him to China where he studied with Master Ju-ching of the Ts'ao-tung school (Soto in Japanese). Here he discovered the original teachings of Hui-neng (the Sixth Zen Patriarch) that za-zen was not just sitting quietly but an actual conscious opening up of oneself to an experience of true reality. Dogen later taught that za-zen is not a meditational practice in which the sitter waits for enlightenment, but that the sitting is of itself an expression of innate Buddha-nature. In his teachings this idea is simultaneously coupled with a complete faith by the practitioner that without striving he or she will, when the time is right, experience in its totality the fullness of pure Buddha-nature. Hence, enlightenment is not something to strive for in a conscious way since this will have a retrogressive effect. Only mental and physical silence produces the transparency in being that provides the right conditions for an illuminating experience of Buddha-nature.

Thus za-zan is not just being seated physically but also mentally. Za is the physical part of sitting, the physical posture. The Zen part is the settling or sitting of the mind. Hui-neng taught that Za was when external objects no longer cause the thoughts to run or the mind to busy itself. That is, in practical terms, that we remain calm in spite of external events. Zen is to see into one's own true nature and for this experience of truth to remain completely in one's understanding even in the middle of inner turmoil and passion.

Dogen returned to Japan and, contrary to traditional practices, he returned empty-handed, carrying no sacred objects or translations of new sutras. He took with him instead a conviction in the power of za-zen as a tool for experiencing enlightenment. He believed that man is already enlightened, that we are all liberated equally but that we do not realize it. Dogen also placed great emphasis on the detail of daily activities and saw each moment as an opportunity to express gratitude for our Buddha-nature. He acknowledged the value of koan practice but not to the extent of the Rinzai school.

In 1236 Dogen started his own temple and his reputation and stature as a religious teacher grew and grew. Today he is revered as one of Japan's greatest historical figures. Dogen would have nothing to do with the military or aristocratic power struggles of his day and this, combined with his belief in the efficacy of physical work, resulted in Soto Zen becoming the Zen of the people. Today Soto Zen is still seen as the school of Zen most likely to attract the non-intellectual.

Beginning za-zen

Times of practice It is best to practise za-zen at a regular time or times every day. Early morning, noon, early evening and before going to bed are the best times. If you can only find time for one session, a morning sitting is the one to aim for. If you wish to sit twice a day, the morning and before bedtime sittings are the best. To begin with fifteen to twenty minutes is enough. Build up to thirty minutes to an hour, depending on your particular situation. I discuss posture below but to start with you can use a chair or stool or halfway through a sitting change to a chair or stool to give aching knees, ankles, etc., a rest. Remember, however, that the quickest way to get a posture you can hold for a reasonable length of time is to stay in it through the discomfort. But, having said that, exercise in moderation.

Posture There are a number of postures that can be used and you should try each of them to discover which suits you best. This does not mean that you should not persevere with one of the more stable postures because it seems, at first testing, uncomfortable. Patience and practice are needed to get good posture.

The recommended postures are described here in increasing order of their stability, balance and conduciveness to good practice. It is perfectly acceptable to start with posture 1 and very few people can sit in posture 5. In all postures the ideal is to sit such that the body is perfectly upright so that a vertical line can be drawn from the centre of your forehead, nose, chin, throat and navel. This is achieved by pushing the waist forward and the abdomen out. In this position the weight of the body is focused on the belly or lower abdomen. This area is the focus of za-zen breathing and concentration. Eyes are half open and focused on the ground about 3–6 feet (1–2 metres) in front of you. In some schools of Zen it is also allowable to keep the eyes closed (as long as you do not doze off!).

Posture 1 This posture is for people who are very stiff through lack of exercise or because of age. Sit facing a blank wall on a stool or chair that is of a height that allows you to set your feet firmly on the ground. If you are tall, adjust your height with a firm cushion on the seat or, if small, a thick plank of wood on

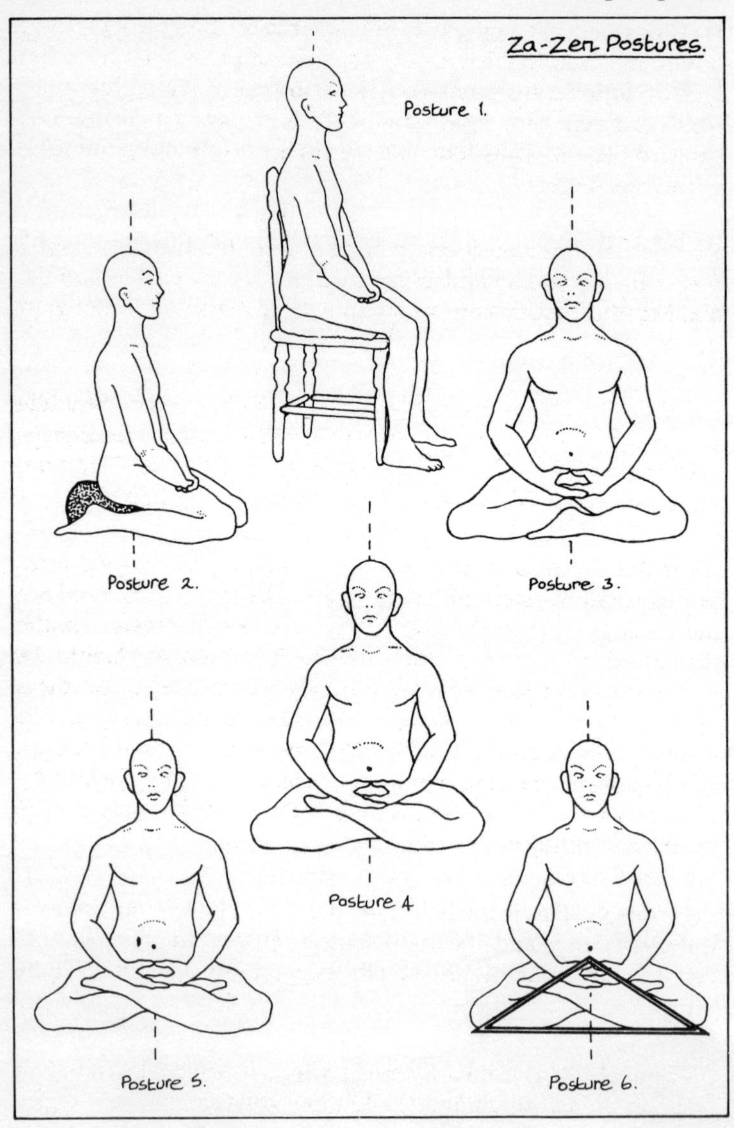
Za-Zen Postures.
Posture 1.
Posture 2.
Posture 3.
Posture 4
Posture 5.
Posture 6.

the floor beneath your feet. Set your back straight, shoulders down and head held upright, not stiff, more as though a thin line of cotton runs from your head to the ceiling. Rest your hands on your lap, right hand under left hand, palms turned upward. The thumbs touch at the tips and form a parallel line with your fingers.

For the next four positions you need a folded blanket about 3 feet (1 metre) square and a firm cushion. Set the cushion on the blanket; the postures are taken up with the cushion under your bottom.

Posture 2 This is the easiest position for beginners. Straddle the mat so that you are sitting on your knees, shins and insteps and bottom. A triangle is formed by your knees and bottom. Head, shoulder and hands are the same as in position 1.

Posture 3 This is the Burmese position, a posture most popular with Western followers of Zen. The legs are crossed but both feet are flat on the blanket. The bottom is situated on the first third to a half of the cushion. Both knees should be touching the blanket. If they are not you may help get them down by putting a second cushion under your bottom or you can place a small cushion under the knee or knees that stick up. It is important to be sitting on a firm base, formed by the triangle of your knees and bottom. Head, shoulders and hands are the same as in position 1.

Posture 4 This is the half-lotus position. The left foot is under the right thigh and the right foot is on the left thigh or vice versa. Both variations are equally as good. This posture is quite difficult for the beginner.

Posture 5 This is the full lotus position in which the right foot rests on the left thigh and the left foot rests on the right thigh. The lotus is the best and strongest sitting position since it forms a perfect triangle between the knees and bottom and produces great stability. Unfortunately, the lotus is also the most difficult posture to achieve and usually out of reach of the beginner and even many mature students. Do not worry if you cannot 'do a lotus' – most of us are in the same position.

Counting breaths

After getting into a good posture to help focus attention the usual practice for beginners is to start counting breaths. To begin with in your practice you can count the in-breaths and the out-breaths. Thus as you inhale count one and as you exhale count two. The count can be audible but later it should be inaudible. As you are counting you will have some thought or other. If this catches you, you will not realize you have been caught up until suddenly you return to yourself. At this point you start concentrating on counting breaths again, beginning at one. If you can reach ten without an interfering thought, go back to one and start again. Do not be surprised if it takes a lot of practice before you can control your mind to concentrate only on your breaths. Incidentally, be sure not to force your breath. Just watch it and count the breaths as they come. After this stage you can start counting only the out-breaths. There is a practice of counting only inhalations but this is not recommended for beginners.

Intermediate za-zen

To move on from the basic za-zen practice (which nevertheless contains much to work on) you will need to find a teacher (see Contact Addresses at the end of the book) or go on to more advanced reading (see A Guide to Further Reading).

Zen in the martial arts

In Japan the essence of Zen is practically experienced in many pursuits such as printing, calligraphy, gardening and the tea ceremony, but particularly in the martial arts. In the past the battle for mastery over oneself and one's weapon, be it sword or bow, had a real life or death meaning on the battlefield.

Nowadays, we choose one of the martial arts as a vehicle through which to develop and express our understanding of the Zen ideal of being able to be totally in the moment, to be at one with Buddha-mind. If we can train our bodies and minds to be in touch with our inner wisdom to rediscover our direct relationship to the cosmic whole, then whatever actions we take will be perfectly suited to the moment. Practice of the martial arts carried out with the right attitude can contribute to the suppleness, openness and trust of body and mind required for such a development. Paradoxically, committed and wise practice of the martial arts leads to a state of being in which one is least likely to need to use in a practical way (against an aggressor) the fruits of one's training. Lao Tzu describes it in the *Tao Te Ching* like so:

> For one in command (of himself) perfection is to be in a position of peace; if he should engage in combat it is without anger; if he should seek to conquer it is without conflict. . . . This is the ideal of a man who will not do battle. It is the art of using human strength by co-operating with the sky (Buddha-Mind – my understanding of sky) and it is the supreme wisdom.

This idea of being in command of oneself is well illustrated in the following story of Tesshu, a nineteenth-century master of fencing and Zen. A young man who was a keen fencer went to see Tesshu and asked him what was the essence of the way of fencing. Tesshu told him to go to Kannon Temple in Asukusa and to pray for the answer to his question. The young man went every day to the temple for a week and prayed for many hours but had no response. He went back to Tesshu and told him but added that on his last day at the temple he had noticed written above the shrine the words 'The Gift of Fearlessness'. Was this anything to do with the answer, he asked. Tesshu replied, 'It is. The secret of our way is complete fearlessness. But it has to be complete. Some there are who are not afraid to face enemies with swords but who cringe before the assaults of passions like greed and delusions like fame. The end of our way of fencing is to have no fear at all when confronting inner enemies as well as outer enemies.'

Thus Zen training in the martial arts has two main aims. The first is to free the mind of the practitioner of ego-centred emotions such as ambition, misplaced competitiveness and fear, and the second is to train the body to move from the instinctive and intuitive centre and not through the intellect. This centre is in the abdomen (*hara* in Japanese) and the Zen martial artist gives over to this centre the command of his movements. Calculated, logically thought-out moves dictated by the intellect are slow in comparison and open to error. By hard and committed training with the right motivation the Zen martial artist strives to become at one with himself and in armed combat at one with his weapon. The difference between technique-orientated and spiritually orientated martial arts is summed up by D. T. Suzuki in this extract from *Zen and Japanese Culture* (Princeton University Press, 1970, p. 146):

> When the sword is in the hands of a technician-swordsman skilled in its use, it is no more than an instrument with no mind of its own. What it does is done mechanically, and there is no (nonintellection) discernible in it. But when the sword is held by the swordsman whose spiritual attainment is such that he holds it as though not holding it, it is identified with the man himself, it acquires a soul, it moves with all the subtleties which have been embedded in him as a swordsman. The man emptied of all thoughts, all emotions originating from fear, all sense of insecurity, all desire to win, is not conscious of using the sword; both man and sword turn into instruments in the hands, as it were, of the unconscious. . . .

Part Two

6 Finding a Club and Dojo Etiquette

Finding a Club

Which martial art?

In the preceding section of the book you will have found brief descriptions of the major martial arts practised in this country. You are now in a position to discover if the one you are interested in really does satisfy your requirements. You may also have come across others with which you are not familiar but which sound as though they may interest you. Remember, however, that no amount of written explanation can do justice to a particular martial art because they all are practical and participatory arts, and participation is the only way you will experience and appreciate the benefits, although, of course, you may be guided by others in your choice.

Obtaining addresses

Having made your decision about a particular style, you are now at the stage of approaching the association concerned in the hope of getting details of clubs in your area. This should be a straightforward matter conducted in the form of a letter or telephone call keeping the contents as simple as possible, for example, your age, experience, health, or anything which may affect your training or progress. (Up-to-date addresses of the various organizations are given at the end of the book.) Take things slowly and enjoy this seeking procedure as the start of your training. If you know of a particular club in your area then a visit is the best approach.

Clubs not listed

The list of organizations given at the end of the book is by no means exhaustive and apologies are extended to those omitted. Note also that a few of the very traditional or ethnic clubs do not like advertising or publicity and their locations are not easily available.

Non-affiliated instructors

There are some instructors who, having been disillusioned or having disagreed with their association, have left and now teach on their own account. Some of these can provide excellent tuition, although you may find amongst them some instructors who do not have appropriate qualifications to teach. Usually instructors within associations have been vetted and accepted.

The instructor's attitude

Deciding whether you will get on with a particular instructor is a difficult judgement for a beginner to make. That is why it is important to visit several clubs and get experience of the different instructors' attitudes. This is best determined by the attitude of his students to one another. This is something which reflects the instructor's approach.

Club atmosphere

Watch out for excessive or uncontrolled aggresion as this may indicate a failing on the instructor's part, although it may be intentional and simply his way of teaching. Be aware also that to the uninitiated some aspects of the martial arts will appear aggressive. Injuries are a sign of uncontrolled techniques. A good technique is controlled and takes into account a person's training, experience and conditioning. A good, friendly but respectful club atmosphere usually means a good instructor.

Instructors' preferences

You will have gathered from the chapters concerning the history of the martial arts and the analysis of their relative practical uses that different styles emphasize particular aspects of physical, mental or spiritual development; thus discover if the club you are visiting fulfils your needs in relation to this. Remember, however, that it is not unusual to find that because of limited time many clubs will not include all aspects of their training on any one night, but usually the instructor will be only too glad to discuss with you his particular interests in the martial arts.

Instructors' qualifications

Again a most difficult task, certificates can be printed to order and possession is no guarantee of proficiency or authenticity. There are many different issuing authorities and you should make some discreet inquiries. No genuine instructor will mind your discussing his qualifications and certificates, although you should always remember that he is not there to be cross-examined – so be polite, explain your difficulty and your wish to be sure that his club is the one you want. This will save you both time eventually.

Facilities

Many martial arts clubs make their home in public sports centres. This is convenient since costs are low and good facilities are provided. Other clubs use church halls and such like where costs are even lower but where only basic facilities exist. Professional instructors or well-established clubs sometimes have their own premises. In these, overheads are high and fees may also be high; however, because they are used solely for club purposes, equipment, mirrors, weights, etc., may be left out for permanent use. Also the club can be used at any time rather than within the limits set in a hired place. Our own view is that the quality of instruction counts more than facilities such as showers and, within reason, costs. One final note, if you join a club that has short-term hired premises do not pay a large membership fee until you are sure of the club's reputation.

Insurance

Most clubs are aware of their liability concerning their students' welfare and take steps to provide suitable insurance protection or can recommend a suitable company with which to obtain special cover.

The Martial Arts Commission insists that all its member associations guarantee that their students are covered by the special insurance cover provided by their own licence. This is available through the parent association.

Besides any cover you may personally take out, most instructors will have public liability insurance cover – satisfy yourself that this is the case; accidents, however unlikely, can prove expensive if wages are lost as a result.

Regular gradings

The progress of students is usually marked with the award of a particular rank after a grading examination has been successfully undertaken, although some clubs practise a system of continuous assessment and others only grade at black-belt level. The regularity of gradings is often an important matter to the student; they should at least be regular enough to ensure that a good student is able to reach first black-belt level after four years' regular training. Note that many students take longer than this because of gaps in the training due to illness, changes of job, and so on.

Dojo Etiquette for Visitors and Students

It is important to appreciate that practitioners of the martial arts take them seriously and that they expect a similar serious attitude from visitors to their club. Instructors will overlook minor infringements of etiquette by visitors and excuse them as acceptable ignorance on their part, but it is still preferable to be acquainted with the more common rules which you are likely to meet whilst visiting different clubs or dojos. When you consider the activities that are practised in the dojo and the dangers associated with them, it is easy to sympathize and appreciate the need for special attention to procedural behaviour.

Common rules

The most common rules you are likely to experience concern bowing on entry to the dojo and removal of shoes in the training area. The bow is not directed to anyone in particular but is part of the ceremonial procedure of separating the outside world from the dojo, and is used as a sign of respect for what one is about to do and of appreciating the dangers and care that must be exercised in it. Removal of your shoes has a more practical reason. Most martial arts are performed in bare feet and thus it is important to take care of the floors, ensuring that no damage ensues and that they are kept clean.

There are many other rules of etiquette, too numerous to mention all of them, but those listed below are most important and most commonly adhered to.

The instructor The instructor is always titled *sensei* in the dojo unless you are told otherwise (this rule fluctuates between dojos but never err on the impolite side!).

Formalities on entering clubs Always bow on entering the training area and to other students whenever training with them. Always return bows from students, although be aware not to waste time making too much of a ritual of this. (Most instructors and students will return bows even if not required to; there are definite times to bow and although you may err on the polite side you must learn when they are necessary – again this varies between dojos.)

Social talking and attention Most classes are formal and social talking is usually kept to a minimum, although there will be time for comment and exchange of views between students. Always be aware of the instructor requiring your attention; time is short and if it is wasted in attracting your attention then you are the loser.

Responding to instructions When the instructor asks you to do something, try to respond quickly. It is part of your training to be aware and to respond as quickly as possible. Follow the instructions carefully and concentrate on what you are doing. Do not make any comment unless one is requested.

Care and cleanliness of equipment For practical, safety and comfort reasons, special clothing and equipment is used in the martial arts (see chapter 4). Always wear the correct clothes in the right way and make sure that they are clean. During training they will get sweaty; fresh sweat smells fine but stale sweat is unpleasant.

Personal hygiene It is important to make sure that your hands and feet are clean; make sure that your nails are short and well scrubbed. If you are unlucky enough to cut someone, it is very unpleasant for them, and increases the danger of infection if your nails are dirty.

Respect

Respect is a word that you will hear again and again in the martial arts and its importance cannot be overemphasized. This is not to say that you should appear excessively humble, more that you should show genuine respect rather than make any pretentious display of it.

Martial arts are exceptionally practical and showing respect is a part of this. Without it there would be no trust between students or between student and instructor and trust is a prerequisite to serious training. You will find that you are expected to take many things on trust during your initial training and respect will help you to do this in instances when you are unable to see the immediate reasons for doing some of the things you are told to do. If you find that you have difficulty developing this trust there may be two reasons. One is that you are not ready to trust and the other is that your instructor has not engendered trust in you. There may be many reasons for either of these problems and it will not always be the instructor's failing.

Changing clubs

As in all aspects of communication and development between teacher and student (particularly development concerning one's own personality and potential), a great deal depends on the compatability of the instructor's methods (including his priorities) with one's own preferences. However, it is important to remember that it is exceptionally difficult for a student to evaluate correctly an instructor and his methods until he or she has had experience of them over a fair period of time.

Be sure that you are making any judgements for the proper reasons, namely, when there are obvious conflicts in attitude, discrepancies between expectations and actual training methods and purposes, or dissatisfaction with the type of tuition provided (see chapter 3). If you are certain that you have made a mistake, then there is no problem in looking for another club, but be sure, take time and try to pinpoint the problem and put it into words. It is most unsatisfactory simply to feel uncomfortable without knowing why and not to benefit from experience. (It is impossible to benefit from any experience if you don't know the problems first!)

Training with others

An important part of your training will involve working with other people and it is possible to become overzealous in this, resulting in injury to either one or both parties. This is a problem that may occur because of pride – one student sometimes quite unintentionally goes a little too hard and the other responds similarly.

Beginners in the martial arts often fail to say when they are being hurt probably because they do not wish to appear less than the image of the strong macho man! Remember that it is quite easy to hurt someone whether you have had training or not. There is no benefit in getting injured so do not suffer silently. A quiet word with your partner (and a short one) is usually sufficient.

No serious injury usually results from overzealousness but bruising occurs. Bruising can stop you training and also puts back any conditioning work you have been doing. It's a nuisance to be avoided. Always be aware of your own and others' capabilities while training (its just as possible to injure yourself or someone else through lack of sensitivity).

7 Progress and Development

Once you begin training in a martial art you will immediately notice the different levels of expertise of the members of your chosen club. The most obvious difference will be that between your own skills and those of the instructor. After you have been training for a while and can start to relax in the club and notice what is going on, you will see that the instructor himself trains, checks his form, is tested by other senior or junior instructors and generally continues to work at improving himself. Herein lies the secret of progress and development – that is, it never stops! Once you have realized this, and do not train with the idea that there is a fixed place to arrive at where you can then rest on your laurels, you can start to train properly. This means training regularly and patiently with no rush and with the awareness that training itself is the target and not the black belt you may aspire to.

Ranks

Different forms of the martial arts use different ranking systems but they all have the same twofold purpose. The first is to give you and other members of the club some idea of your stage of development, and the second is to make it easy for the instructor to divide the class into different ranks for different levels of training. Ranks are awarded after grading examinations (discussed below) and they are usually denoted by the colour of the belt you wear and/or the number of coloured stripes on the belt. In many systems there are ten kyu ranks (below black belt), tenth kyu being the lowest rank and first kyu the highest. There are then up to ten black-belt ranks (occasionally more) starting at first-degree black belt (*shodan*), the lowest, going to tenth-degree black belt (*judan*), the highest.

Grading examinations

It is usual for martial arts associations to agree on the specific requirements needed for a particular rank. This is to ensure uniformity between the various clubs of an association. As a further safeguard it is also usual to have instructors from different clubs attend grading sessions. This gives the students an independent assessment as well as allowing the instructors to arrive at a common standard.

In the grading, the student is usually required to perform particular moves, attacks and defences. Both the difficulty of the moves and the way in which they are executed are judged by the examiners. The following points are looked for:

Strength and spirit As a beginner you will be expected to complete the moves, techniques or exercises you are given with the correct form, that is, in exactly the way you have been taught to perform them. The power with which you do the moves will not be important and you may even spoil your form if you put too much strength into the techniques. Later, as you improve and you test for higher grades, you will be expected to continue to show good form but also to demonstrate power and spirit as well. Spirit in this sense means an expression of your involvement and commitment to the techniques you are demonstrating. It is an intangible quality but the examiners will notice if it is lacking. Thus, when you are testing you are aiming to achieve a balance between form and strength combined with a spirited show of confidence and commitment.

Form Much of your martial arts training will be devoted to achieving good form. By this is meant the ability to execute techniques with precision, power and a perfect harmony of stance, posture and balance. All these qualities must develop in unison since power without precision means no control and precision without power means ineffective techniques. Similarly, a poor stance or bad posture and balance will limit your ability to deliver strong techniques. In our experience, many students slow down their development of good form because they initially try to put too much strength into their techniques. It is easier to start the other way round and to put more strength into, say, a good, well-coordinated punch than it is to put good form into a powerful but poorly executed punch.

Understanding

During your training you will be asked to do things in a particular way by your instructor. If you ask him he will give you an explanation about why he wants you to train in this particular way or practise a technique in a specific manner. Initially you may be dissatisfied with the reasons he gives. They may not make sense to you and you may even feel that your progress is being limited by some aspects of your training. Ignore these feelings and persevere; almost certainly through the training you will start to understand the value and reasoning behind what you are doing. Even if, in your judgement, this turns out not to be the case, be sure that in the martial arts we can learn just as much through disappointment as through success.

Physical and mental development

If you are unfit and unused to physical exercise, you will probably end your first martial arts classes with an aching body. However, compensating for this discomfort will be a warm sense of satisfaction.

After a surprisingly short time of hard training the physical demands of the class will become less of a strain and you will be more able to appreciate and enjoy the fine points of the training. This is a time in your training that is most enjoyable. It coincides with your being both physically fit and still full of excitement about this newfound method of self-expression. Soon after this, however, your hitherto noticeable progress will start to slow down. This is a lean time in your training and you may become despondent about your progress. Despite these feelings, as long as you continue to train hard you will, unbeknown to yourself, be developing a deeper understanding than you had before. Unfortunately some students do not recognize this phase for what it is and drop out. Encourage yourself during this patch and ask the instructors and other students to help you reinforce your determination. They will understand since they will have gone or may be going through similar difficult patches themselves (they recur throughout your training). The rewards for perseverance are worth it.

Mind and body development

All that is meant by this terminology at this stage is that you become more mentally aware of your body. You should learn its limits, its requirements and its potential.

Without this awareness students over-extend in some areas, whilst others tend to take things too easily and do not push themselves enough. It is difficult to get the correct combination at first; it is only by working at becoming more aware of your body that you can do it.

By practising and concentrating on particular skills you can develop an awareness which replaces self-conscious deliberation and calculation by instinctive natural responses. The tennis player naturally performs accurate returns of fast deliveries; the snooker player instinctively 'knows' the angle, spin and strength of most shots, and both only use considered calculation for deciding the tactics of the game. Similarly you should develop a natural instinctive set of body responses. You will then know that when you execute a particular technique or set of moves no time will be wasted thinking about how to achieve them. Your mind and body will act in unison to produce the fastest and best technique you are capable of.

8 Preliminary and Maintenance Fitness Work

Why bother?

It may seem strange to consider doing preliminary fitness work before enrolling for a martial arts course. After all, aren't they going to train me? Don't they know the best ways to get raw beginners fit? Well, yes, they do and, no, they don't. In a good club the instructor will know his particular martial art inside out and all the drills necessary to develop the skills he wants. What he won't and can't know are the individual beginner's capabilities and his or her background. If the instructor knows his side of it – his system – then you need to know your side of it – you. The aim of some preliminary work is not just to get you a little more fit and supple but also for you to get to know yourself.

A tremendous number of beginners drop out quite early on in their training, many just after paying high enrolment fees. So much is this the case that many clubs use high enrolment fees and the subsequent dropout rate from beginners to subsidize the regular members. This is as it should be; beginners absorb large amounts of instruction time and then may train for only a fortnight or so. Now, since this happens in the best clubs as well as in the worst, it is not just because the training is poor. Beginners find the exercise, effort and concentration needed in their training daunting and their confidence falls away, especially when they realize that success is not going to be immediate. This is a traditional test of a student's determination. The training hall is a testing place and often everything the beginner does is wrong. He does not stand right, walk right or even breathe right. Much self-confidence and determination are needed to persevere to get the skills and abilities you have chosen to work for.

It is your body that is the instrument you are working with in all the martial arts and there is a distinct need for you to know and experience how it works, responds and improves. You need to have felt the effort, the tiredness and breathlessness of training and how your body will rise to the occasion, alter and grow towards the new movements. To be more fit and supple will also help in reducing some of the effects of the physical efforts of the class so that you can concentrate more on the instruction.

Feeling clumsy and hopeless and the effect that has on your spirit is an intrinsic part of the training in all the martial arts. Placing your confidence in your ability to improve with time and effort is your best response. You can benefit from recognizing that ability in yourself through preliminary training before you enter the dojo.

Before starting on the actual exercises you may wish to read the following chapter on fitness. This chapter gives the physiological background to the exercises and explains why they benefit us.

Note also that the exercises given here, although designed to help the unfit get fit, are also very good for maintaining fitness.

Preliminary training

Here we are aiming to give you a programme of work to begin before enrolment in a martial arts course and perhaps thereafter as a reinforcement to your training. The exercise set given is for a period of about six to eight weeks. It is aimed at getting you to know more about yourself, rather than grind you into the ground or turn you into Tarzan. It is not all that exciting, although if a particular type of exercise is new to you you may find it stimulating. To build your confidence in your possibilities during these preliminary weeks you need to notice yourself changing and know what is doing it – you are. To improve consistently it is best to work three times a week. This is because the stimulatory effects of exercise soon fade and the muscles and the organs need regular reminding of what we want from them. Three days of not working, and your muscles know you were only kidding and start to waste away again. If you exercise regularly then it gets easier, it builds; lay-offs set you back and you feel it.

If you choose to exercise in this way commit yourself to doing it regularly. You will have problems. You will possibly be working by yourself and that is a problem. There is no feedback from others similarly struggling, no encouragement, incitement or competition to hold you to it. All these things, however, await you in the dojo; until then you will need your commitment. In getting to know your body, compete with your previous performances. Incite and encourage yourself to improve – but remember, slow and steady. Build your confidence not on what you can actually do but on your ability to improve. Stay at it.

The will

This is the most important factor. You are working with your will, that is what you are really exercising through working your body and developing it. When you feel your will working on you (not anyone else), then you will have got to the root of your own worth.

Running

We are using running to develop circulation efficiency – that is, aerobic fitness. This should give you stamina and the wind you will need during training sessions. It will develop your lungs and your legs as well. Running has been chosen because in terms of circulation it gives the best results for the time invested. It also requires little equipment. I began running in a pair of old loose pants, a sweatshirt and pumps. The road is outside your door.

For our programme you need to work out in your mind a run of two miles. The best one, if possible, starts at your front door, goes for a mile to some landmark and then back. Clock this with the mileage gauge on a car or, alternatively, walk easily for about twenty mintues to a particular spot and then return. A round trip of thirty-five to forty minutes at an easy pace should be about two miles. This is your course. If you have got a car of your own you can choose an open, pleasant course. The quieter the better to begin with because if you have not run before you will be embarrassed at first. Even nowadays it feels odd to be a runner in a busy street. In the early stages there may be times when you are hanging onto railings or casually leaning against a lamp-post, breathing deeply. At times like these you can do without well-meaning old ladies and inquisitive dogs.

When you have settled on the course, do not change it. You will only be using it for a few weeks and if you keep to the same course the variations in the time are your improvement. Once the course is organized, the next thing is to set your time. The first occasion when you go out, run and walk the course. That is, stop as often as you need, run as much as you want – run as much as you comfortably can. Time what you do; let that be the bottom line of effort.

Set out your days for running evenly through the week (as evenly as three will go into seven). Stick to those days if you possibly can. Run at any time of the day that suits you, but at least an hour and a half after a light meal or two and a half hours after a larger meal. Make up your mind to cover the distance, even if only walking, in your running kit. Always note your time. Do not worry if it fluctuates. The effort of will is to get you out there, not to force the running. Let that come. Just get yourself out there and time what you do each day.

Slowly your times will improve. You will run more and walk less until you can run it all. Of course, it does not finish there; your time will continue to improve. A good time is a seven-minute mile. Any more than that and you are running, not just getting yourself aerobically fit. So fourteen minutes for your two-mile course is an acceptable time which you may not reach in this short preliminary programme. Few raw beginners would. To be able to run two miles three times a week is no mean feat and, depending on what you are used to, you will feel the effects in your everyday activities as well as the training hall.

Even in the beginning the whole course plus shower should

take you under an hour. Do not eat for at least half an hour after a trot. You want the blood to stay with the muscles and not leave for the stomach too soon. Besides, eating too quickly after a run causes indigestion.

Running equipment Good running shoes make life easier. They are expensive but they need not only be used for training nowadays. Try the course initially in loose clothes, good cotton or wool socks and shorts if you have them. If the weather is cold, dress warmly; otherwise if you may need to stop and if you do you will freeze after a few minutes.

The first few times are the worst – uncomfortable. Stay with it, it gets better.

Strengthening exercises

The resistance of weights is the stimulus to our muscles to increase in size and strength. For these preliminary exercises I am assuming that you have no special equipment so we will use only the body's own weight and initially this works very well. When you start exercising you may find that you cannot manage many repetitions of a movement. With regular practice this will change. As we said earlier, the more repetitions (reps) that one does the more the value of the exercise shifts from purely muscle-to-muscle to blood-supply efficiency. As you become stronger, your reps will increase. At a certain point you may wish to add more resistance in the form of weights. This can save time, prevent boredom and focus your work on building muscle. However, body weight was traditionally sufficient resistance in many of the martial arts, gymnastics and most wrestling systems and for our preliminary course this is still the case.

There are three exercises in this strengthening part of the preliminary course. They are the three that you will find incorporated into most martial arts callisthenic programmes because they are extremely effective in strengthening the major areas of the body. The exercises are squats, press-ups and sit-ups. Also included in the programme are two warm-up movements. They will get the blood circulating, and warm and gently stretch and free the muscles.

Warm-ups The first movement loosens and warms the shoulders, arms, back and chest. The second loosens and warms the lower back, hips and legs.

First movement Circling the arms. Start with the arms down, fingers closed into a tight fist and standing with feet about as wide apart as your shoulders so that you are well balanced. Circle the arms, bringing them upwards and crossing them in front of your body to about head height, then out and around to the sides and back to the starting position. You should build up to very fast, fluid and continuous circling, stretching the arms out and back as far as you can reach on each circle. Count each repetition as your arms pass your face. Do twenty-five repetitions.

Now reverse the circling, swinging your arms up outside of your body, crossing and coming down in front of your body to the starting position. Again build up, start slowly circling, increasing the speed, going fast by about the eighth or ninth rep, then try and keep this speed up for all twenty-five spins.

Do not stop between each rep but keep the arms spinning.

Second movement Forward bends, or touching the toes. For this movement the heels are placed close together, the toes spread a little wider apart for balance. From a standing position begin by leaning back from the hips and then come forward and over, stretching out the arms so that the hands touch the floor or your ankles or shins, and then return. When returning, stretch back beyond the vertical and this will bring more of your body into the movement. Keep the legs as straight as possible and bend not from the waist but from the hips. About 5 inches down from the hips are the bony protuberances of the great trochanter. Feel these bones. They are the pivot points for the bend, not the waist, so bend from the hips, keep your back straight for as long as you can on the way down, then bend it to reach out for the floor. Do twenty of these loosely, stretching back as you come up from each bend.

First strengthening exercise Squats. We do squats to build and

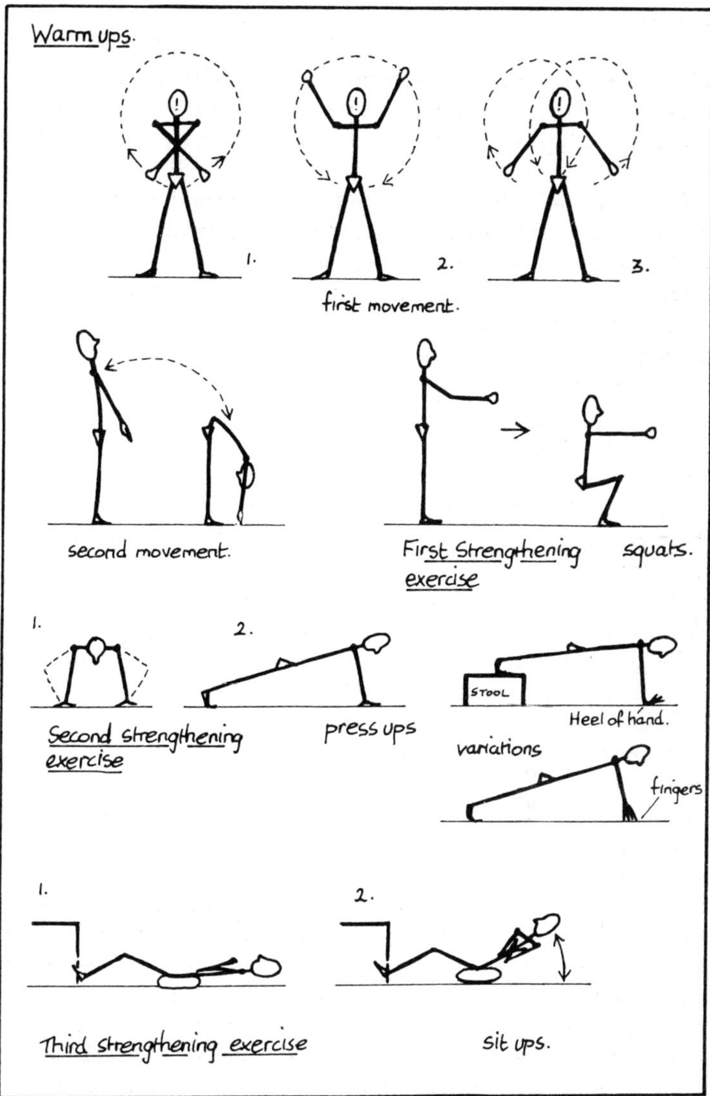
Warm ups.
1.
2.
3.
first movement.
second movement.
First Strengthening exercise
squats.
1.
2.
STOOL
Heel of hand.
Second strengthening exercise
press ups
variations
fingers
1.
2.
Third strengthening exercise
sit ups.

strengthen the legs. They are sometimes called drop kneebends or pliés. Demi or grand pliés are the main leg-strengthening exercises used in ballet. Most weight trainers do squats with a block of wood under their heels, anything from ½–2 inches thick. This throws all the stress onto the large muscles in the front of the thigh. (It can also, however, stress the knee and limit the application of the exercise.) By doing squats with the heels on the floor and keeping them there we develop the hip, inside-thigh, backside and calf muscles as well as the front thighs. The breathing here is very important. With nearly all high-resistance movements, breathe out as you make your effort, in as you return. Breathe deeply, stretching your ribs and diaphragm.

Start with your feet about a shoulder-width apart, feet turned slightly out so as not to twist your knees as you go down. Close your fists, hold your arms out in front of you for balance, bend your knees and drop down as far as you can, keeping both heels down on the floor. Breathe out as you straighten your legs on the return to the standing position. Keep your head up, even look upwards if it helps you to keep your back straight and upright. Do not lean forward; if anything lean back into the movement. Try and do ten repetitions to begin with and then two sets of ten. When this becomes easy increase the number of reps. It is best to do this in groups of five; you'll soon be doing thirty-five, forty reps. Stop at fifty. Two sets of fifty reps is a good level to maintain and will be sufficient for you to see the difference in your legs. Rest for three minutes between sets.

Second strengthening exercise Press-ups. These are to strengthen the shoulders, arms and chest. Many people know this exercise well. There are several versions of it but I only describe a basic form here. That is, to rest the weight of the body on the hands and toes, facing downwards (see illustration). The hands should be just a little wider apart than your shoulders. This hand position is important, so rest on one knee until you have it right and comfortable, not too wide or too close, and not too far towards the head or too far back towards the waist. Bending at the elbows, lower the body down to the ground until the chest touches the floor. The body and legs stay straight throughout the movement. The breath is exhaled as the arms are straightened and the body lifted back. The effort should be felt in the arms and across the chest and shoulders. Start with ten reps. If you cannot manage ten, start with five. Two sets of ten reps should soon be within your capabilities. As you grow stronger increase this by twos and threes up to a limit of thirty reps. Give yourself two minutes between sets.

To vary the effort of this exercise other than by increasing the number of reps try raising the feet on a low stool. This has the effect of increasing the resistance and the angle of effort. Another variation often used in karate is to rest only the fingers on the ground and not the heel of the hand. Resting only on the fingers or even on four, three, or two fingers (including the thumb) obviously strengthens the wrist and fingers but it also raises the body several inches, adding a greater range to the movement and hence effort and stretch to the chest.

Third strengthening exercise Sit-ups. This exercise is for the stomach area and will affect the legs and lower back. It requires equipment in the form of a heavy chair or bed under which you can hook your feet. The chair or bed should not lift when you make your effort in the movement. You may also need a cushion to plant under your backside. The cushion not only prevents chaffing but also raises your hips a little, resulting in more stretch on your stomach as you lower yourself back.

Start by sitting on the cushion with the feet trapped loosely under the chair or bed. To begin with, clasp your arms and hands to your chest. Later as you improve you can clasp your hands behind your head to increase the effort and the stretch. The movement is a short one, only an arc of about 30 degrees from the horizontal to the end position. This is about a third of the full distance to your knees. You will be able to feel the effort go out of the movement at about this point as the muscles, although still moving, are no longer lifting. Start from this 30-degree upright position with your stomach tense and lower yourself back, breathing out, until head and shoulders touch the floor. Then lift back to starting position, exhaling as you go.

Start with ten reps; take several breaths if you need to. Build it up to thirty reps. Do two sets and allow only one minute between sets.

That is the strengthening workout. It is not long. It starts within your capabilities and ends at a very good standard. It requires very little equipment, just loose clothes, trainers or bare feet, a warm room and a heavy piece of furniture. It should not take you more than twenty minutes to do and leads on naturally to the following stretches and suppling exercises. Try it; it will work if you do.

Stretching (yoga) exercises

Following straight on from the strengthening exercises is a good time to do the stretching movements since your body is well warmed up.

Your body is warm and your muscles have been worked but they can get cold rapidly. Draughts in particular cause problems and you will soon start to cool if you sit in one. Thus for these exercises dress in warm loose clothes.

In contrast to a warm body, to stretch properly you need a cool, clear head. These movements are taken up slowly and held with the attention focused on what you are doing. They involve feeling the effects of the pose and constantly relaxing and stretching the muscles involved. They are exterior positions and should be approached slowly. To be effective they must be at the limit of how far you can move in a particular direction. Not that this should hurt. That means you are going too far. Just enough discomfort to let you know that the muscles are being asked to go farther than they normally do is enough. If it is painful, the body's own reflexes will tense to protect the joints affected. This will nullify the benefits of the exercise. So do not bounce into the stretches; hold them and try to relax. The discomfort should then disappear and you may be able to go farther, gently, even if it is only a quarter of an inch.

Start by holding the poses for a count of 20. Then increase this to a count of 60. About one minute is a good length to work towards. If your breath has calmed sufficiently from the previous strengthening work then count breaths instead of plain counting. Three slow breaths to begin with, working up to eight slow deep breaths after a few weeks.

To start with, do these exercises in the sequence given. After a

The stretching (Yoga) exercises.
1.
2.
Straight leg stretch.
Spread leg stretch.
Forward bend.
Cobra stretch.
1.
2.
Back bend.

few weeks you may rearrange the order but stay with these poses. Their effect takes time to penetrate and work into the body.

Shoes may be a hindrance in these poses.

Single-leg stretch Stretch to both sides, stretching from the hips not the waist. Begin by holding the ankle; progress to holding the ball of the foot. Your head moves slowly down to the knee as you loosen up. Do not force the movement but constantly keep stretching into it.

Spread-leg stretch Have your legs spread as wide as you can. Stretch forward. Again stretch from the hips so you are rotating the whole pelvis forwards as you stretch over and down. Stretch to get your head between your legs to the floor.

Forward bend Here we are aiming to get the head down onto the knees. Again, with the feet almost together, start by taking hold of the ankles. Move on to holding the balls of your feet as this brings the calves, ankles and feet into the stretch.

Cobra stretch Start this one lying on your face, then raise yourself up and back. Tilt your head right back as if you are looking at the ceiling. The thighs stay on the floor. The backside and feet are relaxed, loose. Come down very slowly from this pose by lowering yourself on your arms.

Back bend Start with the first posture (1), holding your feet and stretching the hips up as high as you can get them, feet flat on the ground. Try not to let your heels rise. Progress to (2), hands placed close to shoulders, fingers pointing forwards. Feet and hands should be spaced about a shoulder-width apart, with your feet close to your backside and your hands under your shoulders. Lift yourself up, try to straighten your arms and legs, stretch up, let your head curve back under as if you are trying to look directly at the floor. You will need a good foot grip for this pose. Putting your toes against the wall or gripping the floor covering with bare feet are the best.

This is a tough pose; it involves most of the body and is well worth working towards.

The strengthening and stretching exercises are meant to be done together in that they complement each other. Together they will take you about half an hour. If you are very stiff you may try the stretches twice a day for a while.

Start by doing the strengthening and stretching exercises three times a week on alternate days to your run. Later you may wish to do these exercises before your run or do the strengthening exercises before and the stretches after.

This is not a tremendous workout, but it is enough to get you in shape and educate you about how your body works. Also look closely at your diet. You need the right bricks to build your new body with (see chapter 10). Work steadily because what you build slowly lasts longer. It influences different levels of you.

Good luck.

9 Fitness

What is fitness?

Fitness is one of those general, very vague terms that we all use without being really sure what we mean by it. We need to be very clear about what fitness is if we decide to work towards it, and then we can sort out how to become fit and how to know when we have arrived.

Our ideas of fit and unfit are generally to do with how we cope with a particular physical activity and from this experience we decide whether we are fit or not. We all know some 'fit' people and some 'unfit' people, but it is very interesting to see just what criteria we are using to judge them by. We may consider someone fit because he cycles to work. Someone else we call unfit because he wheezes and puffs at the top of a flight of stairs. However, what about the keen amateur footballer who jogs and trains regularly but who continually has a running nose, hacking cough and a bad back. Is he fit?

Sometimes at the top of a flight of stairs we feel fit and strong. On another occasion, say after bursting a collar button trying to move a piano, we can feel definitely out of condition. It is not impossible for both situations to happen on the same day. Thus fitness is not really a general or vague quality, it is a very specific one. When we say the word 'fit' we need to know – fit for what? This is reflected medically in the many different tests for different functions of the body such as muscular strength, heartbeat, blood pressure, oxygen use. These tests are not describing a general physical state, but only one part of that body. To add further to the difficulties of assessing fitness, so interdependent are the various functions of our bodies that often an infirm or weak part will be compensated for by other organs and systems.

Fitness and health

Thus we need to make a distinction between fitness and health. An international gymnast was found to have tuberculosis of the lung while at the height of his career, so it is possible, although unusual, to be fit and ill at one and the same time. Fitness is the body's adjustment or adaption to a particular set of activities. We are therefore only fit for specific tasks. Health is the general ability to fulfil all the daily activities we set our bodies. This involves thousands of functions from the large down to the microscopic, the breakdown of which cause disease. Activities we do regularly our bodies will adjust to and accommodate, even if these include a ten-mile run. However, something unusual for us, such as lifting a piano or dancing the pasadoble, will often catch our bodies unaware and find us lacking in 'fitness'. We can be fit enough to pass several fitness tests and yet still be ill if the illness had not attacked the functions required for those tests.

Thus it is impossible to be perfectly physically fit. Or, for that matter, completely healthy. Fitness is adapting to specific requirements and no one has the time or the inclination to train for all the things that can be tested. Health is a result of the body's incredible ability to balance its multitude of functions, but at any one time something will be wrong, too much or too little, as the body corrects, counter-corrects, stresses or unstresses various parts to normalize itself. This constantly moving balance is called homeostasis. By homeostasis the body is able to maintain itself against climate, infection, stress and dietary changes.

The circulatory system

The circulatory system is one of the chief homeostatic agents of the body. It is the conveyor of all nutritional, respiratory and hormonal substances and is the agent that supplies and cleanses our tissues. Its efficiency is vital to us. Under stress such as exercise or often in illness it is disturbances to the circulation pattern that first inform our awareness that something intense is going on somewhere. This is the pounding in the chest and panting or dizziness as the blood responds to the needs of the various tissues and organs. Some doctors believe that circulatory and lung efficiency may help deal with infection and disease by enabling the body to respond quicker and with greater reserves and supplies of nutriment, oxygen and antibodies. Thus tests of circulatory efficiency come closest to assessing our 'fitness' at being able to respond to a wide variety of stressful activities with the least disturbance to our sense of wellbeing.

Below we give a table which you can use to judge your own

Harvard Step-Up Test*

Using a bench or stool 16–20 inches high, the idea of the test is to step up and down for as long as you can, but for not more than 5 minutes. Try to keep to about 30 complete steps per minute, alternating legs as you wish. When you stop, note the amount of time achieved. Rest for a complete minute, then count your heartbeats for 30 seconds. To find out your score, read off the duration of your effort against the heartbeats counted.

Duration of effort (minutes)	*Heartbeat count for the 30 seconds*										
	40–44	*45–49*	*50–54*	*55–59*	*60–64*	*65–69*	*70–74*	*75–79*	*80–84*	*85–89*	*90–up*
0.00–0.29	5	5	5	5	5	5	5	5	5	5	5
0.30–0.59	20	15	15	15	15	10	10	10	10	10	10
1.00–1.29	30	30	25	25	20	20	20	20	15	15	15
1.30–1.59	45	40	40	35	30	30	25	25	25	20	20
2.00–2.29	60	50	45	45	40	35	35	30	30	30	25
2.30–2.59	70	65	60	55	50	45	40	40	35	35	35
3.00–3.29	85	75	70	60	55	55	50	45	45	40	40
3.30–3.59	100	85	80	70	65	60	55	55	50	45	45
4.00–4.29	110	100	90	80	75	70	65	60	55	55	50
4.30–4.59	125	110	100	90	85	75	70	65	60	60	55
5.00	130	115	105	95	90	80	75	70	65	65	60

Scores: below 50 – poor
50–80 – average
80 and above – good

* From Karpovich, *Physiology of Muscular Activity*, 1959.

circulatory efficiency. It is based on the Harvard Step-Up Test. This test measures the time the pulse rate takes to return to normal after a stressful activity. It measures how long the heart needs to replenish used materials before it can return to a resting rate of heartbeat.

In the rest of this chapter we discuss the various methods for getting fit and the different aspects of getting fit.

Aerobic and anaerobic fitness

The heart is the one muscle that is involved in all our physical activities and it is a general guide to our fitness. However hard we are working, there is always plenty of oxygen in our lungs. The problem is getting this oxygen from the lungs to the muscles. This process is absolutely important in any activity that goes on long enough for us to need an immediate supply of oxygen to the muscles from the air we breathe. Short-term effort can be supplied by the blood's oxygen content without it needing to take on more from the lungs. The ability to sustain effort that requires the blood to absorb oxygen and get it to the working muscles is called aerobic fitness. This is the fitness of long-distance runners, swimmers, mountaineers, etc. There is another type of fitness – anaerobic fitness – which involves short-term rapid explosive effort which burns up tremendous stores of energy; it exhausts the oxygen already present both in the blood and the tissues themselves. This is the fitness of weight lifters and sprinters. Such athletes build up an oxygen debt in their effort; they overdraw on their bloodstream and then collapse in a breathless heap, unable to move another inch until they have repaid that debt. Many sprinters will not breathe during a 100-metre race. In contrast, long-distance runners rely not upon an oxygen debt but upon an efficient system of oxygen taken up by the lungs, transmission of this by the blood and efficient use by the muscles.

Most sports require both aerobic and anaerobic fitness and this is true of the martial arts since they involve long hours of continuous activity with bursts of powerful strenuous effort (such as in fight situations).

Strength

Strength is a separate function from circulatory fitness. True, the heart is involved, but unless the activity is repeated for a period of time the effect on the circulation is very small. This is why we can nip up flights of stairs and may still not be able to shift that blasted piano. Or vice versa, of course. Strength depends upon the size and contraction power of the muscles. It is the size and tone of the muscles, not their strength, that gives the shape and posture that we look for in fit people. Large muscular bodies are really only satisfying to see and have little psychological or aesthetic justification; they also have little value for our health in the general sense. In fact, the extreme development of strength achieved by some weight trainers is often criticized for its detrimental effects on blood pressure and for the strain it puts on the heart in supplying blood to these vast shapes. The aerobically fit marathon runner may look like a plucked chicken – many do. Sprinters and weight trainers have terrific power which shows in their shape but no endurance and little heart efficiency. The martial arts demand both types of fitness to varying degrees because they draw upon the whole of the physical frame and call for both sustained and explosive effort. Notwithstanding this, the sense of psychological wellbeing that we can get from feeling physically strong and well proportioned can be an important contribution to our overall health and confidence just so long as we do not take it too far.

Strength improvement

Training the muscles is a very ancient art; for thousands of years man has studied how to train the human body to carry heavy weights. A famous example is that of Milo of Crotona who was able to lift and carry a four-year-old bull because he had 'trained' to do so by carrying it every day from the time it was a calf. This slow development is still the secret of strength improvement and growth; size and strength go together in the muscles. The muscles must be regularly pitted against a resistance, a resistance that increases and matches the muscles' strength. The muscles obviously respond to function, and regular heavy work soon increases their size and tone. This is due to the body overcompensating for the destruction of muscular components during exercise. Throughout nature, strain – the result of stress – is a direct stimulus to growth. Its effect is obvious in the muscles, but bones, connective tissues and blood vessels all increase and grow as well. This stress and strain should be only just enough to stimulate growth and no more, since damage is done by too much stress and this impedes growth. The resistance should increase very gradually; there is evidence to suggest that strength acquired slowly lasts longer if training should cease. Note, however, that the shorter the extent of the activity the more localized the benefit. Thus single weight-lifting repetitions increase muscle-fibre size and energy store while higher multiples of repetitions also increase the number of capillaries. Exercise with weights undertaken regularly three times a week will show an increase in strength and a noticeable increase in muscle size and tone in two months. A lot of the effect of weights comes from being able to increase them gradually and to be able to see the improvement. It is very important, as we stressed earlier in this chapter, to see yourself improving with your efforts, knowing you are not wasting time. It is that feedback which you need to reinforce and which will keep you coming back to the training. Bear this in mind in any training that you do since you need to know you are succeeding. Slow and steady is the way to do it.

Isometrics

There are ways other than weight lifting of exercising one's strength and thereby increasing it. One is to push against an immovable object. In this way the resistance always matches the effort. This method is called isometric contraction. Many metal-rod and spring devices utilize this form of exercise. The limbs do not move but push against an unyielding resistance. Science has found it effective in increasing strength, but practically it is very difficult to keep up interest in the daily regimes that this type of training requires. It is a handy way to train but only in conjunction with other forms of movement and resistance work. I do not know of anyone using it exclusively with any great success. In the martial arts there are several practices which use muscle opposition to develop strength. This is the isometric exercise of pitting one muscle or, usually, group of muscles against its opposite group. For example, trying to bend the arm and straighten it at the same time. In this exercise both the biceps muscle and the triceps muscle are pushing against a resistance which will increase as both strengthen. In some martial arts exercises this opposition will be extended over the whole body as in the katas of karate. Here there is no boredom involved in building up strength since the interest centres on doing the kata well and the whole exercise is channelled towards a goal. It is worth remembering that all exercise involves weight resistance – sit-ups and push-ups, for example, and even running, for in running we lift and lower our bodies some 1500 times in a mile.

Muscle growth

Muscles grow and hence get stronger by each muscle fibre expanding and by all the fibres starting to work. We only have a certain number of fibres and these we are born with: exercise causes them to grow, store energy and to build strong connective tissue. To grow they need protein in the diet. We discuss this later in the book (see Chapter 10).

When muscles are worked hard they at first get sore. This is usually caused by a build-up of waste products in the muscles which causes irritation. A little very light movement later that same day or next day helps relieve some of this soreness. Severe soreness needs rest but it usually only results from very violent exercise. Too much heavy work too often is self-defeating; it means you cannot train again for days, maybe even weeks. Muscle damage can take a long time to heal. A friend of mine with a torn ligament was in pain from it for about two years. It severely limited his training. Such injuries are rare, but train intelligently and aim for continuous, not rapid, improvement.

Suppleness

Suppleness is the third component of fitness required for the martial arts. The speed and suppleness of martial arts exponents is legendary. The speed they develop is a result of the strength of their blood supply and the flexibility of the nervous system brought about by constant repetition of moves. The suppleness is produced using muscle-lengthening exercises. Muscles are trained not only to contract strongly but also to stretch freely. Suppleness is required for almost all the movements and techniques of the martial arts but it also is often the most demoralizing part of the training for a beginner. You can imagine yourself getting stronger but will your arms and legs ever bend like that?

Callisthenics

Callisthenics are the traditional method of improving suppleness and flexibility. They are used in the preparatory drill-type movements often used at the beginning of a martial arts class. Callisthenics warm up the body, get the blood moving efficiently into and through various muscle groups and build up strength and stretch in the muscles. If used regularly, they increase the range, strength and speed of the movements. Like most exercises, they are weight moving, the weight here being your own body-weight. Repetitions and duration give the strength and blood-supply components of the exercise. The length and range of movements usually demand full use of shoulders, hips, back, etc. This is the flexibility component of the movement, encouraging the muscles to lengthen and loosen. To be effective these movements should cover the widest range of body areas – neck, hips, shoulders, spine, wrists and ankles. Muscles only move freely when warm, so to increase suppleness callisthenic exercises should be started lightly and increased in vigour as the body loosens and begins to free itself. This is important; it is very easy to tear a cold muscle. Flexibility will also be increased if stretching exercises are repeated later on in the session when the body is thoroughly warm.

Stretching

There is little scientific data explaining the benefits of stretching although the sense of wellbeing we feel from it is immediately noticeable. It seems to me that stretching exercises also give balance to the nervous system and feedback which helps give self-control and precision to our movements. The known benefits are that, in lengthening the muscle, the muscle fibres slide over each other to their full extent, helping to flush them with blood and lymph. Stretching exercises also increase the elastic response of the muscle; the fully stretched muscle contracts faster and more strongly from the stretch than it would normally. Many of the movements in the martial arts use this function. The postures and stances give an inherent stretch to muscles which can then rapidly contract into a spring, a kick or a punch. The karate punch is a good example of this action. The fist stretched, tucked and twisted back is able to power foward like a coiled spring. The greater the stretch, the more impetus to the blow.

Hence many of the stances, postures and blows of the martial arts cannot be attained without a good degree of flexibility. Freedom of movement adds greater range, reach and effectiveness in the combat situation. If we compare a martial artist with, say, a boxer, the unpredictability and range of possibilities of his attacks rests on the greater flexibility of his movements.

Most martial arts use callisthenics to develop suppleness (as well as strength and endurance) but they are not necessarily the most effective way of obtaining real flexibility and looseness. Callisthenics involve bouncing into a stretch and out again. This may jar the muscles and often it is better to hold a steady position and allow the muscles to accommodate to the stretch and lengthen fully. This brings us to yoga.

Yoga

The best approach to flexibility is through yoga postures. I would recommend them for any person who finds parts of his body stubbornly stiff. The holding of the posture while the muscle relaxes gradually frees the area. Gradually – a tiny bit every time. Little and often is the way to work. To work on an area, hold the associated posture for up to a minute two or three times a day. It will loosen. It is a very effective method used in many sports. I know several aerobic trainers who use yoga postures to loosen stiff muscles but never mention this to their students. Once gained, the suppleness is relatively easy to maintain by exercising in this way two or three times a week. These postures are also ideal to help alleviate soreness in training. They help balance the whole feel of the body, relaxing and calming. Work them in gently; coax the muscles to stretch, relax and stretch; do not force it, do not rush. Let your body loosen; it takes time, but it works.

Conclusion In the preceding sections I have shown that fitness is a very specific state and should really be qualified by the question 'fit for what?' Thus, as you get better at your particular martial art, you will be specializing your body more and more for that specific style. Note, however, that the martial arts require a wide category of fitness because of the range of skills that they demand of the practitioner.

You will find some of the martial arts stress some of the fitness attributes we have spoken of and play down others. Some, for example, kendo, stress speed and precision; weapons generally do as well. Others, such as judo, have more emphasis on body weight and strength. Even so, within each art are found all types of people emphasizing or compensating for their natural endowments and doing very well, thank you. You think this bulky bloke will be slow, or again this slim one fast but weak, and oh, what a surprise you can get! So in your training compensate for your deficiencies; you will soon learn what they are.

10 Nutrition and Diet

If you start training regularly you may discover, in terms of putting on weight, that you do not need to be so careful about what you eat. At the same time, because training makes you more aware of your body's needs, you may, paradoxically, decide to take more care over your diet. The workings of the body are complex and nutrition is a controversial subject but two facts about diet are quite clear. First, for an overweight but otherwise healthy person, exercise is a more efficient and longer lasting way of losing weight than dieting. Secondly, the fitter we are and the more in tune with our bodies we are, the more care we will take over our diets. The effects of overdrinking, smoking and too much junk food will be experienced more severely and more quickly by the fit person than the unfit. This is one reason, of course, why some people choose to stay unfit. Alternatively, if you choose to stay fit and eat sensibly then you are more likely to be healthy, enjoy a sense of wellbeing, have more energy and live longer.

Below I give a short description of each of the major nutrient groups, followed by general rules for a healthy diet. Much of the information below comes from my book, *Protein-Balanced Vegetarian Cookery* (Rider, 1985).

Proteins, carbohydrates, fats, vitamins and minerals

For growth, maintenance, energy, repair and regulation of

metabolic processes the body needs proteins, carbohydrates, fats, vitamins and minerals. For a healthy and energy-giving diet all five groups are needed in the right balance. Proteins are needed for growth, repair and maintenance of bodily tissues. Carbohydrates and fats provide energy for the body's activities, and fats are also the source of the fat-soluble vitamins A, D, E and K. Vitamins and minerals are required in very small amounts but they are essential to the right functioning and regulation of all the body's processes.

Proteins The proteins the body needs are composed of twenty-two amino acids. Eight of these acids, called the essential amino acids (EAA) cannot be synthesized by the body and must be supplied in the food we eat. All eight essential amino acids are required simultaneously and each must be in the correct proportion to the others if the body is to use them most efficiently. Fortunately for us, food proteins normally contain all eight EAA, although sometimes one or more may only be present in a disproportionately small amount. This small amount of one amino acid limits the usable amount of the remaining essential amino acids since the body must be provided with them all at the same time in exactly the correct profile. The EAA in short supply is called the limiting EAA.

In animal foods the EAA are often present in good combinations and thus their biological value (the percentage of protein present that the body can utilize) is high; however, for the reasons which follow I would recommend that animal protein contributes less to your diet than is usual for people in the West. (In Eastern cooking, meat in small amounts is generally a supplement to grains and vegetables rather than the main course.)

The meat and poultry we usually buy has been reared in poor conditions; it has been fed foods rich in chemicals, many containing hormones, and is high in saturated fat content (although poultry less so than beef, pork or lamb). Notwithstanding this, if you enjoy meat and can afford it, then eaten in moderation it will contribute protein to your diet. Also the metabolism of certain people works best on a diet containing some meat.

Fish is an even better source of protein than meat; they

contain less fat and much of that is unsaturated. Unfortunately much of the sea and many rivers and lakes are polluted and overfished. Thus, for health and ecological reasons I would eat only small amounts of fish and definitely not shellfish which collect and concentrate the pollutants present in the water in which they live.

Plant foods such as grains and beans are also excellent sources of protein as well as vitamins and minerals. Many of them, however, lack one or more of the essential amino acids needed to give them a very high biological value. Fortunately, the amino acid in short supply in one plant food is often available in excess in another and vice versa. By combining two or more complementary plant foods in one meal we obtain protein of much higher quality or biological value than the sum total obtained from eating the foods separately. For example, most grains (e.g. rice, wheat, corn) or grain products are high in the amino acid tryptophan but low in lysine, while most pulses (e.g. beans, peas, lentils) are high in lysine and low in tryptophan. Thus a dish containing, say, rice and lentils will supply protein of a higher biological value than the same total weight of rice or lentils on their own.

Dairy products such as milk, cheese and eggs are also good sources of protein, although as with meat foods they often contain quite a lot of saturated fats and, in the case of eggs, cholesterol. Thus, eat them in moderation and where possible buy low-fat products such as skimmed milk or cottage cheese.

The main sources of non-meat or fish protein are grains, pulses, milk, milk products (e.g. cheese, yoghurt), eggs, nuts and seeds.

The combinations of these food groups which advantageously complement their individual biological values are given below:

1. Milk, cheese, yoghurt or other milk products whether in or with any dish containing grains, pulses, nuts or seeds.
2. Grains either whole or as a flour product either in or with any dish containing pulses or dairy products.
3. Pulses either in or with any dish containing grains, dairy products or nuts and seeds.
4. Small amounts of meat or fish added to any of the plant food protein sources will add significantly to their biological value.

See the following table for the biological table of various food groups.

Table 1 Biological Value of Particular Foodstuffs*

Food group	Biological value (percentage of protein usable by the body)
Ideal protein	100
Whole egg	95
Milk	80–85
Cheese	70–75
Mixed diet of whole grains, pulses, dairy products, nuts and seeds	70–75
Meat (muscle)	70–75
Brown rice	70–75
Whole wheat	65–70
Maize (corn)	50–60
Wheat flour (white)	50
Pulses	40–60
Nuts and seeds	35–55

* Remember these figures only consider protein content. They do not take into account fat, fibre, vitamin, mineral or carbohydrate content.

Carbohydrates Carbohydrates are the body's main source of energy. They are present in foods as starches and sugars. Starch is obtained from cereal grains and their products, pulses, vegetables, especially root vegetables, and nuts. The complex combination of starches and protein in these foods is a good one for people involved in manual work or sporting effort. Naturally occurring sugars are found in fruit, honey and milk. Refined sugar, added liberally to so many foods, should be used moderately. It lacks every nutrient except carbohydrate and it tends to displace from the diet, by spoiling the appetite, other foods containing the nutrients we need.

Fats Fats provide a concentrated energy source and the essential fat-soluble vitamins A, D and E. Every fat or oil contains active (unsaturated) or inactive (saturated) acids or both. The active acids are called essential fatty acids (EFA). They are contained in the polyunsaturated fats recommended by many authorities over saturated fats as a precaution against heart disease. The saturated fats generally come from animal sources such as meat, butter, cream or cheese. Thus, where there is a choice, use vegetable oils such as sunflower, olive, safflower and sesame seed oils, polyunsaturated margarines and low-fat cheeses or other milk products in your cooking. I would also recommend that fats of any description be used in only moderate amounts, particularly saturated fats. There is now a considerable body of opinion that the risk of heart disease, high blood pressure and some cancers can be reduced by cutting saturated fat intake.

Vitamins and minerals The body cannot synthesize the vitamins and minerals it requires and they must be supplied in the food we eat. The vitamins and minerals are an unrelated group of substances but their functions in the body are interrelated and they are all required in the right balance. A mixed diet of whole grains, pulses, dairy products, vegetables, including salads and fresh fruit, plus, where desired, small amounts of meat and fish, will normally provide all the vitamins and minerals we need.

Fibre Fibre is found in unrefined cereals, fruit and vegetables. It is not a nutrient because it is not digested, but because it adds bulk to the body's waste products it is essential to efficient elimination.

General rules for a healthy diet

Moderation and awareness of your own needs are the touchstones of a good diet. As a starting-off point, until you get a balance just right for you, a varied diet of natural foods composed of whole grains or whole-grain products, fresh vegetables and fruit, small amounts of meat, fish and poultry, dried (not tinned) pulses, unhydrogenated vegetable oils, nuts, seeds and dairy products in moderation will supply all the nutrients you need. Natural foods taste better than refined foods and their nutrient and fibre content is always higher. A diet composed mainly of refined foods, often full of sugar and additives, saturated fats and too much salt is definitely bad for your health.

As a general guide, the main meal of the day should provide approximately 50 per cent of the protein you need, one light meal should provide about 25 per cent and breakfast about 25 per cent. Each meal should contain two or more major protein sources and one or more meals should include two or more lightly cooked fresh vegetables and a fresh salad (including a leafy green vegetable). Fresh fruit, including citrus fruit, three or four times a day completes your body's requirements.

In conclusion, you are the best judge of what is the best diet for you. If it keeps you in good health and gives you the energy to do what you want to do, then it is the right diet for your needs.

11 Competition Karate

History

Competition karate fighting was originally devised as a means of pitting the skills of one karate fighter against another. The techniques were meant to be controlled since the 'killing techniques' developed through years of karate training are obviously dangerous if delivered to an opponent full force. Originally a two-tier method of scoring was used in which, depending on the technique, half or whole points were awarded.

Wazari (½ point) This was the technique which beat your opponent's guard and hit the target but which was not delivered with enough power to stop him.

Ippon (1 point) This was a technique which, if it had been delivered full force, would have been a stopping blow.

In the original contests, one ippon, two wazaris or a wazari followed by an ippon were needed to win a match.

In these competitions no body or head contact was allowed and this led to confusing decisions by referees. The fights took on the appearance of ballet battles. This has now been changed and controlled body and head contact is allowed. These changes have led to more exciting and skilful matches.

Modern types of competition

One-point competition In this type of competition one ippon or two wazari techniques win the match. Light facial contact and controlled body contact are allowed. (The controlled body contact can be quite forceful.)

Ways of scoring wazari A punch or kick to the head or body delivered without perfect timing or power.

Ways of scoring ippon

1. A punch to the head or body or a kick to the body which is delivered with perfect power or timing.
2. A controlled kick to the head which lands clean.
3. A foot sweep with a punch or kick follow-up.
4. A technique which turns your opponent around, followed by a punch delivered (with control) to the unguarded back.

The one-point competition is that most commonly found on the open circuit. These are the competitions which are advertised in martial arts magazines and in which affiliation to a governing body is not a necessary criterion for entry.

Three-point competition This system was devised to make competition more sportslike and to make matches longer than the one-point system. Six wazaris, three ippons or a combination of wazaris and ippons which takes the winner up to the three points are needed to win. The three-point system is used for national and international competitions. Competitors have to be members of the governing body of their particular style which itself has to be recognized by a national governing body.

Semi-contact competition Semi-contact competition is a new development which is growing in popularity on the open circuit. It uses an open-ended scoring system or a ten-point maximum.

Point scoring is as follows:

1 point – punch to the body or head with control
2 points – kick to the body or a sweep
3 points – kick to the head or sweep with follow-through
5 points – jumping kick to the head

In semi-contact competition no Japanese terminology is used and the referees use English only.

To add up the points of the competitors, the referees hold adding clickers, one in each hand, and they 'click' up the points as they see them. The points of each referee are added up and the fighter with the most points is the winner. Full body contact is sometimes allowed and as the fighting is continuous the fighters should prepare well especially for stamina.

Knockdown competition In this style of competition full-contact kicks are allowed to all parts of the body except the head, joints and groin. Full-contact punches are allowed to the body but not to the head. If a fighter knocks down his opponent with a strong technique he wins. If no knockdown is scored the referees give a decision as to the superior fighter.

Weight categories at competitions

To avoid unfair matching, competitors are divided into different categories. The division depends on the style of the competition and categories can be made according to weight, grade, age, height and sex, or any combination of these groups.

Weight categories At different competitions at national level any one of these three weight category divisions may be in use:

less than 65 kg 65–75 kg over 75 kg
less than 70 kg 70–80 kg over 80 kg
less than 65 kg 65–80 kg over 80 kg

For ladies only one set of divisions is used at both national and international level. This is:

less than 53 kg 53–60 kg over 60 kg

Seven weight categories are used for men's international competitions. These are less than 60 kg, 60–65 kg, 65–70 kg, 70–75 kg, 75–80 kg, over 80 kg, and open weight.

Normally if weight categories are used in a competition there is no further separation into karate grades. Thus you can have white belts fighting black belts, for instance.

Karate rank categories

In some competitions competitors are grouped not only by

weight but by their karate rank. The types of division used in these competitions are numerous and depend totally upon the individual organizers. Third kyu and above for senior competition and fourth kyu and below for junior (grade) are the most common. There is, however, sometimes an extra beginner category added for the eight to sixth-kyu rank students.

Age categories

In competitions in which contestants are split into age categories there is normally no division into grades. At national and international level the junior division is for fighters aged between sixteen and twenty-one. There is then a further division by weight.

The beginner and competition karate

Free fighting is a part of karate which is included in every student's training. The amount of emphasis placed on free fighting totally depends on the individual instructor. If during your training you find that free fighting is the part of training that gives you the most pleasure, then you could have the potential necessary to become a good competition fighter. Speak to your instructor about it. If you dislike free fighting, do not avoid it, try to improve your free fighting as you would improve your kata. However, you will probably not have the mental attitude needed to be a good competition fighter.

Preparation for competition

As a beginner it is necessary to get your basic techniques correct (not perfect). The techniques I would suggest to start practising are:

1. Reverse punch (with your best hand) off the back leg.
2. Back fist or lunge punch using the leading hand.
3. Front kick off the rear leg.
4. Roundhouse kick off both the front leg and the rear leg.

These four techniques can be expanded and improved upon as your skills improve. Distance, power and control can be developed by punching and kicking a bag or impact pad. Once the basics have been developed you are ready to start putting your skills to use in free fighting with a partner. Free fighting helps with movement, blocking, distance and timing, and when done for sustained periods improves stamina. Once you have confidence in your free-fighting ability, and it is most important that you are confident, you are ready to start competing.

To begin with, start fighting for points in the confines of your own club. A marked-out fighting area helps to add tension, which is something you must learn to deal with. If you are fighting for points for the first time, do not forget about your control. This is the first discipline you must learn and the easiest one to lose.

You may well begin to feel that you are ready for your first competition, but before entering I would suggest you go along and watch one. Find a suitable competition such as those advertized in martial arts magazines. Contact the organizer and ask him or her to send you application forms. Check the forms and see if there is a category that would suit you. If there is then go along to the competition and watch; do not enter. Pay attention to your category and try to gauge how well you think you would do if you were down there competing. If you go and watch the competition and feel you would like to be down there fighting, this is a good sign. It shows you have the hunger for competition. Once you are ready, enter a competition and see how it goes.

Try to learn from your own mistakes and from watching other fighters who are better than you. Two points to remember; enjoy yourself and always fight to win.

How to get into the national squad

If your club is a member of the national governing body then your instructor will be notified of National B-squad training sessions. These are open to all but you should be a reasonably good fighter before you consider going to one of the selection meetings. Weight categories are used to divide fighters into groups. If you perform well at one of the B-squad sessions you could be selected for the A squad. You will then be eligible to represent your country.

Part Three

A Guide to Further Reading

The following list of books is intended for those readers who may wish to find out more about the technique, history and background of the martial arts. While it is not possible to learn a complex skill such as a martial art from a book, there is no doubt that the information contained in these works will help to make certain aspects of training more understandable for a beginner. More advanced students can also benefit by observing variations on techniques they may already know.

The list is in no way exhaustive, nor is it intended to be; space considerations have meant that some very valuable works have not been included. All the books listed are in English or contain substantial English sections, and for the most part should be available from martial arts supply companies or bookshops. One or two books are now quite rare, but should be available through inter-library loan. Wherever possible publishing details are supplied.

History, Philosophy and Training Methods

P. L. Cuyler, *Sumo: From Rite to Sport*, Weatherhill, New York, 1979.
T. Deshimaru, *The Zen Way to the Martial Arts*, Rider, 1983.
D. F. Draeger, *The Martial Arts and Ways of Japan*, 3 vols., Weatherhill,

New York, 1973, 1974.
D. F. Draeger, *Weapons and Fighting Arts of the Indonesian Archipelago*, Tuttle, Vermont, 1972.
D. F. Draeger and R. W. Smith, *Asian Fighting Arts*, Ward Lock & Co., 1970.
M. Finn, *Iaido: The Way of the Sword*, Paul H. Crompton, 1982.
G. Funakoshi, *Karate-do: My Way of Life*, Kodansha International, Tokyo, 1975.
V. Harris, *A Book of Five Rings*, Allison & Busby, 1974.
E. J. Harrison, *The Fighting Spirit of Japan*, T. Fisher Unwin, 1913.
E. Herrigel, *Zen in the Art of Archery*, Routledge & Kegan Paul, 1953.
H. Kauz, *The Martial Spirit*, Overlook Press, New York, 1977.
R. Kim, *The Classical Man*, Masters Publications, 1982.
R. Kim, *The Weaponless Warriors*, Ohara Publications, Burbank, California, 1974.
T. Leggett, *Encounters in Yoga and Zen*, Routledge & Kegan Paul, 1982.
R. Marchini and L. Fong, *Power Training in Kung-Fu and Karate*, Ohara Publications, 1974.
I. Nitobe, *Bushido, the Soul of Japan*, Tuttle, 1969.
R. Otake, *The Deity and the Sword*, 3 vols., Minato Research & Publishing Co., 1977.
M. Oyama, *The Kyokushin Way: Mas Oyamas Karate Philosophy*, Japan Publications Inc., 1979.
N. Perrin, *Giving up the Gun: Japan's Reversion to the Sword 1543–1879*, David R. Godine, Boston, 1979.
M. Random, *The Martial Arts*, Octopus Books, 1978.
H. Reid and M. Croucher, *The Way of the Warrior: The Paradox of The Martial Arts*, Century Publishing, 1983.
A. Sollier and Z. Gyorbiro, *Japanese Archery: Zen in Action*, Weatherhill, New York, 1969.
R. Storry, *The Way of the Samurai*, Orbis Publishing, 1978.
S. R. Turnbull, *The Book of the Samurai: The Warrior Class of Japan*, Arms & Armour Press, 1982.
B. Wallace, *Dynamic Stretching and Kicking*, Unique Publications, 1981.
G. Warner and D. F. Draeger, *Japanese Swordsmanship: Technique and Practice*, Weatherhill, New York, 1982.
A. Watts, *Tao: the Watercourse Way*, Pantheon Books, 1975.
W. S. Wilson; *Ideals of the Sumurai*, Ohara Publications, 1982.

Zen and the Martial Arts

A. Bancroft, *Zen, Direct Pointing at Reality*, Thames & Hudson, 1979.
J. Blofeld, *The Zen Teaching of Huang Po*, The Buddhist Society, London, 1968.
R. H. Blyth, *Zen and the Zen Classics*, Hokuseido Press, Tokyo, 1962.

H. Dumoulin, *Zen Enlightenment*, Weatherhill, New York, 1979.
Fung Yu Lan, *The Spirit of Chinese Philosophy*, Routledge & Kegan Paul, 1962.
C. Humphreys, *Zen Buddhism*, Heinemann, 1949.
T. Leggett, *Zen and the Ways*, Routledge & Kegan Paul, 1978.
R. Linssen, *Zen, The Art of Life*, Pyramid, New York, 1969.
I. Schloegl, *The Zen Way*, Sheldon Press, 1977.
K. Sekida, *Zen Training*, Weatherhill, New York, 1975.
D. T. Suzuki, *An Introduction to Zen Buddhism*, Rider, 1969.
D. T. Suzuki, *Manual of Zen Buddhism*, Rider, 1950.
D. T. Suzuki, *Zen and Japanese Culture*, Princeton University Press, 1970.
S. Suzuki, *Zen Mind Beginners' Mind*, Weatherhill, New York, 1970.
A. W. Watts, *The Way of Zen*, Thames & Hudson, 1960.

Martial Arts of the World

Japanese/Okinawan karate

Shotokan

K. Enoeda, *Shotokan Kata*, 2 vols., Dragon Books, 1983.
G. Funakoshi, *Karate-Do Kyohan: The Master Text*, Kodansha International, Tokyo, 1973.
H. Kanazawa, *Shotokan Karate International Kata*, 2 vols., Tokyo, 1981.
H. Kanazawa and N. Adamou, *Kanazawa's Karate*, Dragon Books, 1981.
M. Nakayama, *Best Karate*, 8 vols., Kodansha International, 1977–81.
M. Nakayama, *Dynamic Karate*, Kodansha International, 1966.
H. Nishiyama and R. C. Brown, *Karate: The Art of Empty-Hand Fighting*, Tuttle, Vermont, 1959.

Wado Ryu

S. Ohgami, *Introduction to Karate*, Japanska Magasinet, Göteborg, 1984.
S. Ohgami, *Karate Katas of Wado Ryu*, Japanska Magasinet, 1981.
T. Suzuki, *Karate-Do*, Pelham Books, 1967.

Kyokushinkai

H. Collins, *The Kyokushinkai Knockdown Karate Book*, Collpet, 1980.
B. Fitkin, *Kyokushinkai Karate Kata Book*, Sweden, 1980.
M. Oyama, *Advanced Karate*, Japan Publications Inc., 1970.
M. Oyama, *This is Karate*, Japan Publications Inc., 1965.
M. Oyama, *What is Karate?*, Japan Publications Inc., 1966.

Shito Ryu/Shukokai

T. Morris, *Shukokai Karate Kata*, Paul H. Crompton, 1982.
Y. Nanbu, *Sankukai Karate*, Habitex Books, Cambridge, Ontario, 1974.

N. Omi, H. Okubo and K. Tomiyama, *Tani-Ha Shito-Ryu Katas*, Paris, 1982.
R. Sakagami, *Karate-Do Taikan Pinan*, Kyusei Inc., Tokyo, 1974.
C. Tani, *Karate-Do*, Tani Karate Research Institute, Kobe, Japan, 1977.

Uechi-Ryu

G. Mattson, *Uechi Ryu Karate-Do*, Peabody Publishing Co., Newton, Massachusetts, 1974.
G. Mattson, *The Way of Karate*, Tuttle, Vermont, 1963.

Shorin Ryu

C. Motobu, *Okinawan Kempo: Karate-jutsu on Kumite*, Ryukyu Imports Inc., 1977.
S. Nagamine, *The Essence of Okinawan Karate-Do*, Tuttle, Vermont, 1976.
T. Yamashita, *Shorin Ryu Karate*, Ohara Publications, Burbank, California, 1976.

Isshin Ryu

S. Armstrong, *Seisan Kata of Isshinryu Karate*, Ohara Publications, 1973.
H. Long and A. Wheeler, *Dynamics of Isshinryu Karate*, 3 vols., National Paperback Book Co., Noxville, Tennessee, 1978, 1980.

Goju Ryu

S. Toguchi, *Okinawan Goju Ryu*, Ohara Publications, Burbank, California, 1976.
Gogen Yamaguchi, *Karate: Goju Ryu by the Cat*, International Karate-Do Goju Kai, Tokyo, 1966.
Gosei Yamaguchi, *Goju Ryu Karate*, 2 vols., Ohara Publications, 1972, 1974.

Okinawan weapons

F. Demura, *Bo: Karate Weapon of Self-Defense*, Ohara Publications, Burbank, California, 1976.
F. Demura, *Nunchaku: Karate Weapon of Self-Defense*, Ohara Publications, 1971.
F. Demura, *Sai: Karate Weapon of Self-Defense*, Ohara Publications, 1974.
F. Demura, *Tonfa: Karate Weapon of Self-Defense*, Ohara Publications, 1982.
M. Inoue, *Ancient Martial Arts of the Ryukyu Islands:* 1. *Bo*; 2. *Sai*; 3. *Nunchaku*; 4. *Tonfa*, Seitosha Co. Ltd, 1976–78.
R. Sakagami, *Nunchaku and Sai: Ancient Okinawan Martial Arts*, Japan Publications Inc., 1974.

Chinese systems

J. Cheng, *Wing Chun*, Paul H. Crompton, 1977.
C. Cheng Leong and D. F. Draeger, *Phoenix Eye Fist: A Shaolin Fighting Art of South China*, Weatherhill, New York, 1977.
P. Chye Khim and D. F. Draeger, *Shaolin: An Introduction to Lohan Fighting Techniques*, Tuttle, Vermont, 1979.
T. L. Fong, *Choy Lay Fut Kung-Fu*, Ohara Publications, 1972.
Y. Jwing-ming, *Shaolin Chin Na: The Seizing Art of Kung-Fu*, Unique Publications, 1980.
Y. Jwing-ming and J. A. Bolt, *Shaolin Long Fist Kung-Fu*, Unique Publications, 1981.
T. Khek Kiong , D. F. Draeger and Q. T. G. Chambers, *Shantung Black Tiger: A Shaolin Fighting Art of North China*, Weatherhill, New York, 1976.
B. Kong and E. H. Ho, *Hung Gar Kung-Fu*, Ohara Publications, 1973.
C. Man-ch'ing and R. W. Smith, *T'ai Chi: The Supreme Ultimate Exercise for Health, Sport and Self-Defense*, Tuttle, 1967.
R. W. Smith, *Chinese Boxing Masters and Methods*, Kodansha International, 1974.
R. W. Smith, *Hsing-I: Chinese Mind-Body Boxing*, Kodansha International, 1974.
R. W. Smith, *Pa Kua: Chinese Boxing for Fitness and Self-Defense*, Kodansha International, 1967.
L. Ting, *Wing Tsun Kuen*, International Wing Tsun Leung Ting Martial Art Association, Hong Kong, 1978.

Korean systems

H. Cho, *Korean Karate Free-Fighting Techniques*, Tuttle, 1968.
H. I. Cho, *Man of Contrasts*, Cho's Taekwondo Center, Los Angeles, 1977.
H. H. Choi, *Taekwondo: The Art of Self-Defence*, Daeha Publication Company, Seoul, 1965.
R. Chun, *Moo Duk Kwan Taekwondo*, Ohara Publications, 1975.
B. S. Han, *Hapkido: Korean Art of Self-Defense*, Ohara Publications, 1974.
B. S. Huan, *Taekwondo*, Russ International, Singapore, 1975.
J. M. Jee, *Hapkido*, 2 vols., International Hapkido Association, Pasadena, California, 1973.
S. D. Kang, *One Step Sparring*, Ohara Publications, 1978.
C. Norris, *Winning Tournament Karate*, Ohara Publications, 1975.

Kickboxing/full-contact karate

M. Gyi, *Burmese Bando Boxing*, American Bando Association, 1978.

B. Lee, *Tao of Jeet Kune Do*, Ohara Publications, 1975.
B. Lee and M. Ueyhara, *Bruce Lee's Fighting Method*, 4 vols., Ohara Publications, 1976, 1977.
H. Stockman, *Kickboxing: Muay Thai*, Ohara Publications, 1976.
S. Tanjaworn, *Thai Boxing: The Devastating Fighting Art of Thailand*, Divine Wind Inc., Mountain View, California, 1975.
B. Urquidez, *Training and Fighting Skills*, Unique Publications, 1980.
D. F. Warrener, *Full-Contact Martial Arts*, Paul H. Crompton, 1978.

Indonesian, Malay and Filipino systems

H. Alexander, Q. Chambers and D. F. Draeger, *Pentjak-Silat: The Indonesian Fighting Art*, Kodansha International, 1970.
Q. Chambers and D. F. Draeger, *Javanese Silat*, Kodansha International, 1978.
D. Inosanto, *The Filipino Martial Arts*, Know Now Publishing Company, 1977.
R. Latosa, *Escrima*, Wu Shu-Verlag Kernspecht, 1979.
R. Presas, *Modern Arnis: The Filipino Art of Stick Fighting*, Ohara Publications, 1983.

Sport karate

D. Anderson, *American Freestyle Karate: A Guide to Sparring*, Unique Publications, 1980.
V. Charles, *Sport Karate*, Paul H. Crompton, 1982.
D. Valera, *Karate Competition*, Paul H. Crompton, 1973.

Western systems

B. Almeida, *Capoeira: A Brazilian Art Form*, North Atlantic Books, Richmond, California, 1981.
R. G. Allanson-Winn and C. Phillipps-Wolley, *Broadsword and Single-stick*, George Bell & Sons, London, 1890.
S. Andre and N. Fleischer, *A Pictorial History of Boxing*, Hamlyn, 1975.
G. D'Amoric, *Les Boxeurs Français: Treatise on the French Method of the Noble Art of Self-Defence*, London, 1898.
J. Dempsey, *Championship Fighting*, Nicholas Kaye, 1950.
A. Hutton, *The Sword and the Centuries, or Old Sword Days and Old Sword Ways*, 1901; reprinted Tuttle, 1973.
G. Kent, *A Pictorial History of Wrestling*, Spring Books, 1969.
J. Robinson, *Claret and Cross-Buttock, or Rafferty's Prize Fighters*, George Allen & Unwin, 1976.

G. Silver, *Paradoxes of Defence*, Shakespeare Association Facsimile no. 6, Oxford University Press, 1933.

A. Wise, *The History and Art of Personal Combat*, Hugh Evelyn, 1971.

Contact Addresses

This section is divided into two parts. Initially we give addresses for Zen organisations, then the addresses of those martial art organisations affiliated to the Martial Arts Commission (MAC) details of which can be obtained from:

MAC 1st Floor Broadway House, 15/16 Deptford Broadway, London SE8 4PE. (Tel 01 691 3433)

These addresses are kept as up to date as is possible though changes do occur. I am not able nor am I qualified to recommend the clubs and associations listed here, that is not the purpose of this section and even though the MAC do vet their members, attention is drawn to the points mentioned in chapter 6.

In addition to the following addresses, it is worth noting that the Karate Union of Great Britain (KUGB) will provide details of their member clubs (estimated at around – 400 Shotokan style) and these can be obtained from the following contact address:

KUGB Maychalk House, Musters Road, West Bridgeford, Nottingham. (Tel 0602 820757)

Martial Arts Commission

Membership – 1st January 1987

Secretariat Office
Broadway House, 15–16 Deptford Broadway, London, SE8 4PE. Tel: 01-691-3433 – club enquiry line 01-691-8711.
Chairman
Mr B. Whelan, 1 Berwick Place, Coatbridge, Scotland. Tel: 0236-25840.
Vice-Chairman
Mr B. Eustace, 368 Birmingham Road, Stratford Upon Avon, Warwickshire.
Treasurer
Mr E. W. J. Stratton, Meadowside, North Down Road, Bideford, North Devon. Tel: 023-72-76774.
Finance Officer
Mr R. W. Eagle, c/o Eagle & Co., Oakdale Avenue, Pinner Road, Northwood, Middlesex HA6 1PG.
General Secretary
Mrs P. Mitchell.
Acting Asst. Gen. Secretary
Mr R. Thomas.

English Karate Council
Mr D. Bradley, Flat 2, 20 College Park Avenue, Belfast, BT7 1LR. Tel: 0232 238826.
Miss M. Cannon, 8 St Lukes Close, Canvey Island, Essex, SS8 9NF. Tel: 0268 693431.
Mr D. L. Mitchell, PO Box 159, London, SE18 2NH. Tel: 01-855-2633.
Mr J. Kerridge, 51 Palmers Road, Arnos Grove, London, N11 1 RJ. Tel: 01-361-8686.

Scottish Karate Board of Control
Mr D. Bryceland, 74 Lamington Road, Glasgow, Scotland, G52 2SE. Tel: 041-833-6095.
Mr B. Whelan, 1 Berwick Place, Coatbridge, Scotland, Tel: 0236-25840.

Welsh Karate Federation
Mr K. Mumberson, Smalldrink, Parsonage Lane, Begelly, Kilgetty, Dyfed. Tel: 0834-813-776

Northern Ireland Karate Board
Mr D. Redmond, 185 Dunclug Park, Ballymena, Co Antrim, BT43 6NU.
Mr T. Boyle, 52 Raby Street, Ormeau Road, Belfast 2.

British Kung Fu Council
Mr J. Huang, 21 Horsenden Crescent, Sudbury Hill, Middlesex, UB6 0JF. Tel: 01-864-3255.
Mr R. W. Eagle, c/o Eagle & Co., Oakdale Avenue, Pinner Road, Northwood, Middlesex, HA6 1PG.

Observer: Mr R. Smith, 11 Lucas Close, Yateley, Hampshire, GU17 7JD.

British Takewondo Board

Mr R. M. K. Choy, Eastney, 58 Wiltshire Lane, Pinner, Middlesex, HA5 2LU. Tel: 01-863-0664.

Mr J. Ingram, 53 Geary Road, Gladstone Park, London, NW10. Tel: 01-450-3471.

British Jiu Jitsu Association

Mr R. Clark, W J J F, Barlows Lane, Fazakerley, Liverpool 9. Tel: 051-523-9611.

British Aikido Board

Mr B. Eustace, 368 Birmingham Road, Stratford Upon Avon, Warwickshire.

Mr J. Cornish, 109 Greengate Street, London, E13 0BG. Tel: 01-552-7439.

British Kendo Association

Mr R. Schofield, Wenlock Edge, Park Hill, Pilton, Shepton Malett, Somerset, Tel: 0749-89241.

Mrs H. M. Corder, 10 Broad Oaks, Wickford, Essex, Tel: 0268-766060.

British Shorinji Kempo Association

Mr R. Jarman, 31 Fairlawn Grove, Chiswick, London, W4. Tel: 01-994-4324.

Mr P. White, 43 Beauchamp Raod, Sutton, Surrey, SM1 2PY. Tel: 01-642-4056.

U.K. Tang Soo Do Federation

Mr M. K. Loke, 44 Holden Way, Upminster, Essex, Tel: 04022 25739.

U.K. Sul Ki Do Federation

Mr M. Y. Kim, National Sulkido Academy, 1st Floor, 472 Caledonian Road, London, N7 8TB. Tel: 01-607-9517.

British Thai Boxing Federation

Mr J. C. Barker, 63 Carr Meadow, Willow Vale, Clayton Brook, Nr. Preston, PR5 8HR. Tel: 0772 324935.

Nippon Dai Budo Kai

Ms B. Stewart, Nippon Dai Budo Kai, Barlows Lane, Fazakerley, Liverpool, 9. Tel: 051-523-9611.

Associate Member

British Students Karatedo Federation

Mr R. Thomas, 140 Southend Arterial Road, Gidea Park, Romford, Essex, RM2 6PR.

Mr A. MacPherson, The Hospice, Wycombe Abbey, Marlow Hill, High Wycombe, Bucks. Tel: 0494-20387.

English Karate Council

Membership – *as of July 1987*

Secretariat Office
Ms M. Cannon, PO Box 159, London SE18 2NH. Tel: 0268-693431.
President
Mr L. Palmer, 77 Cambridge Road, West Wimbledon, London, SW20 0PU. Tel: 01-947-2000.
Chairman
Mr D. Mitchell, PO Box 159, London, SE18 2NH. Tel: 01-855-2633.
Vice-Chairman
Mr B. Dowler, Walters Fladgate Solicitors, 9 Queen Anne St., London, W1M 0BQ.
Team Manager/Coach
Mr D. Donovan, 133–135 High St. South, East Ham, London, E6. Tel: 01-471-7470.
Chief Referee
Mr B. Smith, 1 Middle Pavement, Nottingham NG1 7DX. Tel: 0602 503756.

Executive Committee

Mr D. Mitchell, PO Box 159, London, SE18 2NH. Tel: 01-855-2633.
Mr. B. Dowler, Walters Fladgate Solicitors, 9 Queen Anne St., London, W1M 0BQ.
Mr M. Higgins, 51 St Johns Road, Erith, Kent, DA8 1PE. Tel: 03224-49558.
Mr J. Kerridge, 51 Palmers Road, Arnos Grove, London, N11 1JR. Tel: 01-361-8686.
Mr S. Rowe, 159 Darnley Road, Strood, Rochester, Kent, ME2 2UH. Tel: 0634 711372.
Mr B. Tatlow, 2 Moat Farm Drive, Bedworth, Warwickshire, Tel: 0203 363959.
Mr D. Bradley, Flat 2, 20 College Park Ave, Belfast, BT7 1LR.
Mr D. Donovan, 133–135 High St South, East Ham, London E6. Tel: 01-471-7470.
Mrs S. Higgins, 51 St Johns Road, Erith, Kent, DA8 1PE. Tel: 03224-49558.
Mr V. Charles, 17 Huntingdon St, London, N1 1BS. Tel: 01-609-3471.
Mr L. Palmer, 77 Cambridge Road, West Wimbledon, London, SW20 0PU. Tel: 01-947-2000.
Mr B. Smith, 1 Middle Pavement, Nottingham, Notts. NG1 7DX. Tel: 0602-503756.
Miss M. Cannon, PO Box 159, London, SE18 2NH. Tel: 0268-693431.

Members Associations/Federations
As at July 1987

1. *Full Members*

Amateur Shotokan Karate Association
Mr D. Martin, 84 Ounsdale Road, Wombourne, Wolverhampton, W. Midlands.
Mr D. Bradley, Flat 2, 20 College Park Ave, Belfast, BT7 1LR.

British Karate Ishin-Ryu
Mr D. Donovan, 133–135 High St South, East Ham, London, E6. Tel: 01-471-7470.

British Karate Union
Mr R. Evans, 'Tresco', 145a Loxley Road, Stratford Upon Avon, Warwickshire.
Mr J. Johal, 32 Palmerston Road, Forest Gate, London, E7. Tel: 01-472-2719.

British Shito-Ryu Karate Association
Mr R. Mills, Henley Management College, Greenlands, Henley on Thames, Oxon RG9 3AU.

Bujinkai Karate Association
Mr J. Smith, Fursdon Leisure Centre, Penrith Gardens, Estover, Plymouth, Devon. Tel: 0752-771711.

English Contact Karate Association
Mr M. Haig, BAI Building, 99 John Bright St, Birmingham, B1 1BE. Tel: 021-643-4270.

English Goju-Ryu Karate-Do Association
Mr G. Malone, 8 Elmbank Ave, Arkley, Barnet, Herts. Tel: 01-499-8997.
Mr G. Andrews, Riverside Cafe, 248 Rotherhithe St, London, SE16. Tel: 01-237-2029.

Federation of English Karate Organisations
Mr J. Kerridge, FEKO, PO Box 821, London, SE8 4PS. Tel: 01-361-8686.
Mr T. Daly, 19 Hermitage Road, Haringay, London, N4 1DF. Tel: 01-800-5419.

International Karate Union
Mr T. Steward, 29 Beaminster Gardens, Barkingside, Essex. Tel: 01-550-1222.

Karate-Do Shotokai
Mr A. Baker, Redcliffe House, 92c Whiteladies Road, Bristol, BS8 2QN. Tel: 0272-743535.

Kenyukai Karate Centres
Mr T. Pottage, 10 Thompson Road, Denton, Manchester, M34 2PR. Tel: 061-336-2824.
Mrs L. Stevens, Kusa Yama, 48 Clifton Drive, Foxlow Park, Buxton, Derby. Tel: 0298-77362.

Kofu-Kan Shito-Ryu Do
Mr T. Murthwaite, 119 Hallfields Road, Gunthorpe, Peterborough. Tel: 0733-72399.

Southern Karate-Do Wadokai
Mr B. Wilkinson, South View, Folly Lane North, Upper Hale, Farnham, Surrey GU9 0HU. Tel: 0252 723622.

Thames Karate International
Mr R. Fuller, 16 Netherwood Court, 1 Lower Park Road, Belvedere, Kent. Tel: 01-384-2498.
Mr R. Colwell, 2 Ribble Road, Gateacre, Liverpool, 25. Tel: 051-428-2686.

United Kingdom Seiki-Jukyu Karate Organisation
Mr F. Perry, Busen, 9 King St, Twickenham, Surrey. Tel: 01-892-3338.

2. *Provisional Members*

British Karate-Jutsu Karate-Do Kai
Mr E. Spencer Brown, 2nd Floor, 26 Lower St, Maidstone, Kent. Tel: 0622-688167.
Mr B. Creton, 54 Albert Road, Folkestone, Kent.

Codrington European Karate Development Organisation
Mr E. Codrington, 18 Handsworth Wood Road, Handsworth Wood, Birmingham, B20 2DS.

Elite Karate Association
Mr J. Johnson, 56 Chetwynd Road, Penn, Wolverhampton. Tel: 0902-334666.

Midlands Karate Federations
Mr S. Darkes, 14 Welford Road, Sutton Coldfield, Warwickshire. Tel: 021-643-3731.

Phoenix Karate Organisation
Mr B. Tatlow, 2 Moat Farm Drive, Bedworth, Warwickshire. Tel: 0203-363959.

Takamizawa Karate Institute
Mr S. Rowe, 159 Darnley Road, Strood, Rochester, Kent, ME2 2UH. Tel: 0634-711372.

United Kingdom All Styles Karate Organisations
Mr R. Stanhope, 9 The Meade, Chorltonville, Manchester, M21 2FA. Tel: 061-860-5255.

United Kingdom Karate Jutsu
Mr B. Dowler, Walters Fladgate Solicitors, 9 Queen Anne St, London, W1M 0BQ.

British All Styles Karate Association
Mr G. Wallace, 619 Romford Road, Manor Park, London, E12 5AD. Tel: 01-552-7335.

Federation of English Karate Organisations

Membership – as of January 1987

Secretariat Office
PO Box 821, London, SE8 4PS.
Chairman
Mr J. Kerridge, 51 Palmers Road, Arnos Grove, London, N11 1RG.
Vice-Chairman
Mr P. Chadwick, 115 Caunce Street, Blackpool, Lancs.
Secretary
Ms J. Sanders, 103 Lexham Gardens, London W8 6JN.
Treasurer
Mr M. Higgins, 51 St Johns Road, Erith, Kent, DA8 1PE.
Chief Referee
Mr. D. James, Greenacres, High Hesket, Carlisle, Cumbria.
National Coach
Mr E. Cox, 50 Cranmore Road, Newbridge, Wolverhampton.
Honorary Vice Presidents
Mr M. Harada, Flat 3, 5 Creffield Road, Ealing, London W5.
Mr T. Morris, 68–74 Glassford Street, Glasgow G1 1UP.
Mr S. Asano, 421 Westdale Lane, Mapperley, Nottingham, NG3 6DH.

Member Associations of the Federation of English Karate Organisations

Amateur Karate Kai
Style: Wado Ryu. Distribution: Midlands.
Mr J. McCann, 47 Patrick Road, Corley, Northants.

Amateur Martial Arts Association
Style Wado Ryu & Shotokan. Distribution: National
Mrs N. Powell, 10 Coppice Close, Stratford on Avon, Warwickshire, CU37 6TN.

Association Of Nippon Kempo
Style: Nipon Kempo. Distribution: London, Liverpool.
Mr L. De Gale, PO Box 92, London, W11 2BG.

British Isles Karate Association
Style: Wado Ryu. Distribution: Lancs, W. Yorkshire and Tyne & Wear.
Mr G. Watkins, 2 Lorne Walk, St Anns, Nottingham, NG3 4FX.

British Karate Association
Style: Free Style. Distribution: Manchester & North.
Mr D. Connor, Oriental World, 18 Swan Street, Manchester.

British Karate Chojinkai
Style: Wado-ryu. Distribution: Cumbria, Cleveland, Tyne & Wear, W. Midlands.
Mr D. A. James, 'Greenacres', High Hesket, Carlisle, Cumbria, CA4 0HU.

British Okinawan Karate Bugeikai
Style: Okinawan Karate. Distribution: Hampshire, Sussex.
Mr R. Woodhams, Greenways, Mill Lane, Titchfield, PO15 5DU.

British Sankukai Karate Association
Style: Sankukai. Distribution: Worcs & Beds.
Mr K. Beddoe, 8 Perrin Avenue, Kidderminster, DY11 6LL.

British Shotokan Karate Shinboku Association
Style: Shotokan. Distribution: National.
Mr C. Mack, 28 Ashburnham Mansions, Ashburnham Road, London SW10.

Bukonkai
Style: Shotokan. Distribution: National.
Mr C. Williams, 49 Kingsway, Newton, Chester.

Bushido-Kai
Style: Shukokai. Distribution: Lancs.
Mr R. Chadwick, 140 Freshfield Avenue, Bolton, BL3 3HL.

England Karatedo Wadokai
Style: Wado Ryu. Distribution: Teeside, Coventry.
Mr W. Seaton, 111 Norton Road, Stockton on Tees, Cleveland.

English Korean Karate Association
Style: Korean Karate. Distribution: Suffolk.
Mr J. Day, 3 Fen Farm Cottages, Washbrook, Ipswich, Suffolk, IP8 3HE.

English Shotokan Karate Association
Style: Shotokan. Distribution: North London, Beds, Essex, Herts.
Mr R. Hall, Flat 5, Elsenham Hall, Elsenham, Bishops Stortford, Herts.

Great Britain Karate Federation
Style: Wado Ryu & Shotokan. Distribution: National.
Mrs I. Haywood, 12 Newhorse Road, Cheslyn Hay, Walsall, Staffs.

Higashi Karate Kai
Style: Wado Ryu. Distribution: National.
Mr P. Whitney, 17 Martinsfield, Covingham, Swindon, Wilts.

International Sankukai Karate Association.
Style: Sankukai. Distribution: Home Counties.
Mr B. Stranack, 12 Monkton Close, Ferndown, Wimborne, BH22 9LL.

In Yo Kan Karate Association
Style: Wado Ryu. Distribution: London & South East.
Ms A. Shortell, 3 Hamilton Road, Southall, Middlesex, UB1 3BQ.

Jin Sei Kai Karate Association
Style: Shotokan (Kanazawa Ryu). Distribution: Hertfordshire, Essex.
Mr P. Perry, 28 Folly Fields, Wheathampstead, Herts.

Kateda School of Self Defence
Style Kateda. Distribution: London & Essex.
Mr P. Davis, 1 Chalford Court, Pershore Close, Barkingside, Essex.

Katsu Karate Federation
Style: Wado Ryu. Distribution: West Midlands.
Mr E. Cox, 50 Cranmore Road, Newbridge, Wolverhampton, W. Midlands.

Northern Karate Association
Style: Shotokan. Distribution: Yorks, Humberside & Newcastle-upon-Tyne.
Miss W. Murton, 1 Denesway, Garforth, Leeds, LS26 2AT.

Sei-Bu-Kan Wado-Kai Association
Style: Wado Ryu & Kempo Karate. Distribution: Hampshire, Devon, Channel Islands.
Mr W. Evans, 100 High Lawn Way, Havant, Hants.

Seishinkai Shotokan Karate
Style: Shotokan. Distribution: Home Counties.
Mr M. Phipps, 34 Crawley Drive, Hemel Hempstead, Herts. HP2 6BS.

Sentenashi Karate Kosai
Style: Anshinryu. Distribution: Co. Durham.
Mr P. Carbert, Sentenashi Karate Centre, 107 Gladstone Street, Darlington.

Shorai karate Association
Style: Shukokai. Distribution: Lancashire.
Mr J. F. Tierney, 8 Armstrong Street, Horwich, Lancashire, BL6 5PW.

Shotokan Karate Association
Style: Shotokan. Distribution: North London, Middlesex, Herts.
Mr M. Randall, 26 Poynter Road, Enfield, Middlesex.
Shotokan Karate Of Great Britain
Style: Shotokan. Distribution: Leicester & Nottingham.
Mr J. Edwards, 31 Howard Close, Loughborough, Leicester.
Shotokan Karate International
Style: Shotokan. Distribution: National.
Mr A. Hampson, 185 Wollaton Road, Beeston, Nottingham.
Shotoryu Karate Kai
Style: Shotoryu. Distribution: North & South Devon & Channel Islands.
Mr M. Crooke, 61 Haddington Road, Stoke, Plymouth, Devon.
Shukokai Karate Federation
Style: Shukokai. Distribution: West Midlands, North West, Guernsey. Dorset.
Mr E. Daniels, Shukokai Karate Centres, 3–5 Park Street, Digbeth, Birmingham.
Mr S. Stewart, 55 Broadstone Road, Bradshaw, Bolton, BL2 4AT.
Sokudo Karate Association
Style: Shukokai. Distribution: N. England.
Mr A. Shaher, 85 Acklam Road, Middlesborough, Cleveland.
South Of England Karate Association
Style: Wado Ryu. Distribution: Surrey, Sussex, Hants.
Mr P. D. Elliott, 54, Billingshurst Road, Broadbridge Heath, Nr. Horsham, Sussex.
South Of England Karate Union
Style: Shotokan. Distribution: South of England.
Mr M. V. O'Donnell, 25 East Street, Porchester, Nr. Fareham, Hants.
Sports Karate Organisation
Style: Free Style. Distribution: London.
Mr D. Mitchell, 38 Bassant Road, Plumstead, London SE18.
Swanda-One Karate Association
Style: Swanda-One. Distribution: Cornwall, Cheshire.
Mr A. Burgoyne, 18 Hollins Road, Macclesfield, Cheshire, SK11 7EA.
Traditional Association of Shotokan Karate
Style: Shotokan. Distribution: Beds, North Herts.
Mr J Van Weenan, Harlington Manor, Harlington, Bedfordshire.
Uechi Ryu Karate Association G.B.
Style: Uechi Ryu. Distribution: Merseyside & Home Counties.
Dr D. L. Scott, 21A Aigburth Drive, Liverpool, L17 4JQ.
Mr T. Daly, 19 Hermitage Road, Haringey, London, N4 1DF.
Unity Self Defence
Style: Self Defence. Distribution: London.
Mr R. McNeil, 3 Colville Houses, London, W11 1JB.
Wessex Karate Association
Style: Wado Ryu. Distribution: South of England.
Mr M. Simpson, 11 Kingston Road, Poole, Dorset.

Zenshin-Do Karate Association
Style: Shotokan. Distribution: Birmingham & West Midlands.
Mrs S. Graham, 10 Endicott Road, Aston, Birmingham.

Provisional Members

British Sports Karate Association
Style: Freestyle. Distribution: London central.
Mr V Charles, 17 Huntingdon St, Barnsbury, London W1 1BS.
Karate Sankukai East Midlands
Style: Sankukai. Distribution: East Midlands.
Mr D. Carruthers, 46 Oakfield St, Stapleford, Nottingham, NG9 8FF.
London Goju Ryu Karate Centre
Style: Goju Ryu. Distribution: Central London.
Mr C. Rowen, 188/94 Old St, London, EC1.
Middlesex Shotokan Karate
Style: Shotokan. Distribution: Hounslow & Isleworth.
Mr E. McGuigan, 12 Albury Ave, Isleworth, Middlesex.
Northern Area Shukokai Karate Association
Style: Shukokai. Distribution: Northern England.
Mr T. Pemberton, 1 Taunton Avenue, Leigh WN7 5PT.
Sanchin Wado Kai
Style: Wado Ryu. Distribution: West Midlands.
Mr L. Service, 20 Haney Hay Road, The Triangle, Chasetown, Burntwood, Walsall, West Midlands.
Shinji-Ryu Karate Association
Style: Shukokai. Distribution: Lancashire, Cheshire.
Mr T. Scott, 5 Sunnybrow Road, Gorton, Manchester, M18 7AE.
Ty Ga Karate Association
Style: Wado Ryu. Distribution: West & SE London.
Mr G. Wasniewski, 58 Kensington Court, London W8.

Satellite Members

Amateur Shotokan Karate Association
Style: Shotokan. Distribution: National.
Mr D. Martin, 84 Dunsdale Road, Wombourne, Wolverhampton, West Midlands, WV5 8BW.
Mr D. Bradley, 5 Brackendale Close, Hounslow, Middlesex, TW3 4AZ.
British American Karate Clubs
Style: Mugendo. Distribution: London.
Mr B. S. Johal, 32 Palmerston Road, Forest Gate, London, E7.
British Karate Ishin Ryu
Style: Ishin Ryu. Distribution: Greater London, Essex.
Mr D. Donovan, 133–135 High Street South, East Ham, London, E6.
English Goju Ryu Karate Association
Style: Goju Ryu. Distribution: S. England, Lancashire, Greater Manchester.
Mr L. Sim, 3 Wisteria Close, Buttercups Estate, Wokingham, Berks.

English Karate Organisation
Style: multi-style. Distribution: National.
Mr R. Evans, 124 Warwick Street, Leamington Spa, Warks, CV32 4QY.

Karatedo Shotokai
Style: Shotokai. Distribution: Birmingham, Bedford, Tyne & Wear, Manchester, Glos, Surrey.
Mr Z. Boban, 13a The Avenue, Old Windsor, Berks SL4 2RS.

Kofu-Kan
Style: Shukokai. Distribution: National
Mr T Murthwaite, 119 Hallfields Lane, Gunthorpe, Peterborough.

Thames Karate - South
Style: Shotokan. Distribution: London & S.E.
Mr R. Fuller, 16 Netherwood Court, 1 Lower Park Road, Belvedere, Kent.

Thames Karate - North
Style: Shotokan. Distribution: Merseyside & Yorks.
Mr. R. Colwell, 2 Ribble Road, Gateacre, Liverpool, 25.

Index